Spring IN *Sicily*

Spring IN Sicily

Food from an Ancient Island

MANUELA DARLING-GANSSER

Photography by Simon Griffiths

Hardie Grant Books

MELBOURNE · LONDON

Acknowledgements

Many people have helped in the production of this book. In particular I would like to thank Vittorio Sportoletti-Baduel, Claudio Biaggi, Giulio and Laura Ripa di Meana and Carla la Rosa for sharing their knowledge of Sicily. Maria Scarf and Ada Stanton helped with recipes.

In Sicily I had generous assistance from Natalia Jung, Alberto Coppola, Antonella Titone, Nardino Argate, Antonio Drago, Angelo and Maria-Concetta Cataldi, Michele Caruso and Carla Rametta, Carlo Hauer, Santo and Franco La Mancusa, Ornella Lucifora, Donato Tetto, Giorgio Cannata, Vincenzo Lo Mauro, Maria Grammatico and Giorgia Colomba.

Klarissa Pfisterer and Hamish Freeman again contributed their exceptional design skills; Julie Pinkham, Catherine Cradwick and Mary Small at Hardie Grant were always supportive and helpful; and Lucy Malouf was a tenacious and knowledgeable editor.

Simon Griffiths again shared his beautiful photographs and Daniel Darling was a great travelling companion when I was researching the book.

Finally my thanks to my family – my children, Miranda, Jason and Daniel, and my husband, Michele. They are my most enthusiastic supporters and my toughest critics.

Published in 2009
by Hardie Grant Books
85 High Street, Prahran, Victoria 3181, Australia
www.hardiegrant.com.au
www.hardiegrant.co.uk

Cataloguing-in-Publication Data is available from the National Library of Australia.

ISBN 978 1 74066 739 5

Edited by Lucy Malouf
Photography by Simon Griffiths
Cover and text design and layout by Pfisterer + Freeman
Colour reproduction by Splitting Image Colour Studio
Printed and bound in China by C&C Offset Printing Co. Ltd

10 9 8 7 6 5 4 3 2 1

www.manuelafoodandtravel.com

Michele

A te che hai preso la mia vita
e ne hai fatto molto di piu

contents

conversion tables

WEIGHT

Metric	Imperial
10–15 g	½ oz
20 g	¾ oz
30 g	1 oz
40 g	1½ oz
50–60 g	2 oz
75 g	2½ oz
80 g	3 oz
100 g	3½ oz
125 g	4 oz
150 g	5 oz
175 g	6 oz
200 g	7 oz
225 g	8 oz
250 g	9 oz
275 g	10 oz
300 g	10½ oz
350 g	12 oz
400 g	14 oz
450 g	1 lb
500 g	1 lb 2 oz
600 g	1 lb 5 oz
650 g	1 lb 7 oz
750 g	1 lb 10 oz
900 g	2 lb
1 kg	2 lb 3 oz

VOLUME

Metric	Imperial
50–60 ml	2 fl oz
75 ml	2½ fl oz
100 ml	3½ fl oz
120 ml	4 fl oz
150 ml	5 fl oz
170 ml	6 fl oz
200 ml	7 fl oz
225 ml	8 fl oz
250 ml	8½ fl oz
300 ml	10 fl oz
400 ml	13 fl oz
500 ml	17 fl oz
600 ml	20 fl oz (1 pint)
750 ml	25 fl oz (1 pint 5 fl oz)
1 litre	34 fl oz (1 pint 14 fl oz)

Note: A pint in the US contains 16 fl oz;
a pint in the UK contains 20 fl oz.

TEASPOONS, TABLESPOONS & CUPS

1 teaspoon	5 ml
1 tablespoon	20 ml
1 cup	250 ml

This book uses metric cup measurements, i.e. **250 ml for 1 cup**; in the US a cup is 8 fl oz, just smaller, and **American cooks should be generous** in their cup measurements; in the UK a cup is 10 fl oz and **British cooks should be scant** with their cup measurements.

TEMPERATURE

C°	F°
140	275
150	300
160	320
170	340
180	350
190	375
200	400
210	410
220	430

LENGTH

Metric	Imperial
5 mm	¼ in
1 cm	½ in
2 cm	¾ in
2.5 cm	1 in
5 cm	2 in
7.5 cm	3 in
10 cm	4 in
15 cm	6 in
20 cm	8 in
30 cm	12 in

introduction

I HAVE BEEN IN LOVE WITH THE ISLAND OF SICILY FOR MOST OF MY LIFE. UNTIL recently I did not know it well, but it has always been there, just on the edge of my mental horizon, a place of mystery and fascination. As a child I went on family summer holidays to the Aeolian Islands off the north coast and I have returned several times since, but only for brief visits that left me wanting more. This book is the result of a long-held ambition to travel the island, to experience the very different landscapes and to thoroughly explore its food and traditions.

The best time to visit Sicily is in the spring. Winter can be cold and grey, while summer is very hot and in autumn the land has a parched, even exhausted appearance. But in springtime the full bounty of growth that this fertile island can produce is on display. Fruit trees and vines are in new leaf, wheat fields stretch to the horizon, and wildflowers grow in profusion along the roadside. At sea, unseen but keenly awaited, tuna are massing for their annual migration along the north coast and swordfish swim in the Straits of Messina. You can see the results of all this abundance in Sicily's famous street markets and in the spring they are dazzling.

There is a great diversity of produce and cooking in Sicily depending on where you go. This should not be surprising as the landscapes on the island are all so different. You find long stretches of coastline, inland valleys and mountains, fertile lava fields and isolated islands.

To this diversity in landscape you have to add layers of history of an extraordinary richness. Situated in the very centre of the Mediterranean with a number of excellent harbours, Sicily has always been strategically important. But it was the harvests of its seas and agriculture that made it particularly attractive. You might say the various conquerors came to occupy – but stayed to enjoy.

Sicily has been settled over the past 2500 years by most of the major players in Mediterranean history. Carthaginians, Greeks, Romans, Moors, Normans and dynasties from France and Spain all saw the island as a prized possession. Even today the remnants of the respective occupations are all around you. In this sense Sicily is something of a living museum – the past is always with you.

Nowhere is this more true than in the food. If you put all the specialties of Sicily on a long table under a pergola (and what better place to enjoy it), you would have the whole history of the island spread before your eyes.

Not all the conquerors had the same impact – some were definitely more civilised than others. One group that left a very strong legacy was the Moors, who ruled the western part of the island in the tenth and eleventh centuries. Their capital, Palermo, was a wonder of the civilised world at the time. And in keeping with their culture, the Moorish influence on food was very strong and is still there today. It is something that makes the food of Sicily distinctive.

The people of Sicily are also one of its attractions. They are a diverse group, with the history of the island quite literally in their DNA. You still often see the blue eyes or the red hair of the Normans, for instance. Sicilians are very aware of their past, still often speak Sicilian dialects among themselves and consider themselves to be different from the 'mainlanders' of Italy.

In more recent times, the island has had bad press when stories about the Mafia and blood feuds hit the news. This has cast a shadow over life in parts of Sicily, but in all my travels I have always felt safe and, almost without exception, I have found the people to be warm and welcoming. In the countryside you may find a natural reservedness, but if you express interest or appreciation in what people are doing, they become open and friendly.

In the cities life is changing. Increasingly you see city centres that look cared-for, with derelict historic buildings being renovated and protected. A new sense of openness and optimism seems to be replacing the old ways. It is as if the island is waking from a long darkness to reclaim its place in the sun.

So you can see why I am so drawn to Sicily. I am passionate about food – and not just the food on the plate. I want to know the history, the traditions and how the various dishes came about. If you understand all this, it adds greatly to your enjoyment of the food itself.

This book is a story of my travels in Sicily and the food that I found. It is not meant to cover everything and go everywhere and the selection is very personal. I have chosen to focus on the places that appealed to me and the recipes that I would cook at home to remind me of my visit. The food is fundamentally Mediterranean Italian (with a strong Sicilian accent), so it is simple, direct, healthy and full of strong flavours – the sort of food we all enjoy today.

So if this is the food you like and Sicily holds the same fascination for you, join me in my travels and sample the wonderful food of this ancient island.

SICILIA

MARIS ME=

DITERRA=

NEI

PARS

N

Mondello

Palermo

Scopello

Erice
Trapani

Favignana

Marsala

Maretimo

Apud Joh. et Cornel. Blaeu.

Palermo
LA CONCA *d'Oro*

TO TRAVEL TO AN ISLAND ALWAYS GIVES THE SENSE OF LEAVING ONE WORLD
and entering another. Even though its northeast coast is within sight of the Italian
mainland, to visit Sicily you need to take a ferry or a plane. Situated in the middle
of the Mediterranean Sea, roughly midway between the east and west, and north
and south coasts, Sicily has a sense of being at the very centre of the Mediterranean.
If you arrive by air from the north, as I did, this sense of journeying to a different
world – a world at the crossroads of history – is all the more real.

But first you must make a choice: where do you begin your trip? Sicily is very
broadly divided between the east (which was Greek in ancient times and later over-
laid with a rich layer of Spanish baroque), and the west and north. Although settled
over the centuries by many occupiers, such as the Carthaginians and Romans, the
west and north were the centre of Moorish rule and this is where their influence is
most pronounced. Palermo was the Moorish capital and today is the island's centre
of regional government. It was in Palermo that I decided to begin my travels.

As your aircraft circles to land, through the window you can see the city's
extraordinary setting. A deep bay lies between two mountain headlands creating

Above: Me and 'my' boat!
Opposite: A view of the
bay at Mondello, a seaside
town just outside Palermo

a splendid natural harbour. Into the bay runs what was once a fertile plain, well watered by rivers coursing down from the mountains behind. Broadly triangular in shape, this plain is the famous Conca d'Oro (literally Horn of Gold – but meaning Horn of Plenty), which has produced agricultural riches for the city of Palermo down the centuries.

Today much of the Conca d'Oro is covered in urban sprawl as the city has burst its bounds to spread inland. You have to use your imagination to see the productive fields of early settlement, the world-famous irrigated gardens of Moorish times or even the botanical pleasure gardens for which Palermo was renowned at the end of the nineteenth century.

I have visited Palermo on several occasions and have always been enchanted. It is a city of enormous vitality and a distinguished, multi-layered history. Wandering the streets you see churches and cathedrals from Norman times, sometimes built on the sites of mosques from an earlier period. There are baroque palazzi, ornate classical and baroque churches and grand buildings from the nineteenth century. Behind the grandeur, in narrow lanes and small squares, are residential buildings,

Above and opposite: Buildings in old Palermo

Above and opposite:
Shops selling bicycles
and kitchen utensils
in Palermo

some quite run-down, that have been lived in for centuries. Here and there are small commercial centres – a street of shops selling bicycles or small workshops selling all sorts of home-made kitchen utensils.

Even on the grand avenues the shops have a rather old-fashioned quality. Instead of the usual array of international luxury brands, you see local retailers selling quite formal clothes of their own making. These are interspersed with good independent bookshops, picture framers or furniture restorers. Today Palermo's agricultural past is only on display at its famous produce markets. The city is now a thriving administrative and commercial centre, a place that is very conscious of its rich history, but where the heritage of the past is worn lightly and the future is very much in people's minds.

Palermo must have originally been settled because of its harbour and good agricultural land. Down the centuries if you occupied good real estate in Sicily you had to be able to defend it. So Palermo must have been a fortified town from its earliest days as it attracted the attentions of Phoenicians, Greeks, Romans, Arabs and Normans.

The golden age of Palermo lasted from the tenth to the twelfth centuries, first as a Moorish capital under Arab rule and then as a Norman kingdom. During this time it was regarded as a jewel of the Mediterranean, a city to rival the great centre of Baghdad far to the east. Under the Moors, the city enjoyed great prosperity, as both the economy and the arts flourished. Although the Norman kings restored Christianity, they were tolerant towards the Muslim population and adopted many of the ways of their predecessors. During this era, Palermo became one of the great commercial and cultural centres of Europe, renowned for its beauty, climate and wealth. It is said that during the rule of King Roger II, his income from the city of Palermo alone was greater than his Norman cousins received from the whole of England.

A lot of this wealth came from the new agricultural practices that were introduced by the Moors in the ninth and tenth centuries. It was probably the Phoenicians who introduced the vine and the olive, about 4000 years ago, but it was the Moors with their sophisticated irrigation techniques who greatly increased the yield of existing crops and were able to grow new plants that needed a reliable supply of water. The Moors brought a whole cornucopia of these new plants with them to

the island. Oranges, lemons, dates, figs, sugarcane, rice, pistachio nuts, carobs and the zibibbo grape were all introduced by the Moors, as well as a taste for drinking coffee. They also brought cotton, papyrus for papermaking and mulberries with silkworms for spinning silk. Later occupiers introduced other plants, particularly the Spanish who brought potatoes, tomatoes, prickly pear and corn from their New World empire.

In modern Palermo, however, it is the Moorish influence that gives Sicilian food its distinctive local character. Spices and herbs like cinnamon, wild fennel and mint are still commonly used. Pine nuts are mixed with raisins in many dishes. But it was the introduction of a new and abundant source of sweetness, sugar, that probably had the greatest influence on Sicilian cuisine. It was from these times that the Sicilians must have acquired their notable sweet tooth.

Foods preserved in vinegar were sweetened to become agro-dolce – sweet and sour – of which the famous local dish caponatina is an example. Marzipan (sugar with almonds), cassata (sugared ricotta) and sorbets (sugared fruit purées mixed with snow) have become emblematic Sicilian delicacies.

Above: At the Vucciria market
Opposite: Buying bottarga (dried, pressed tuna roe)
Following pages: Abundant produce at the Ballarò market

When I arrive in a new city, I like to walk the streets to get a feel for the place and when I do, I am inevitably drawn like a homing pigeon to the produce markets. So on my first morning back in Palermo I set off early to walk around the old centre – and walk you must because driving is only for the locals and the brave. And, as I did, I gravitated to its two famous street markets, the Vucciria and the Ballarò, both near the centre of the old city.

Although it is only a block away from some of Palermo's smartest streets, the Vucciria is in a poor neighbourhood. The market stalls line a small square and the street that runs through it. Even though it is a fairly humble market, it has great character and the produce on display, whether in the market stalls or a few specialty shops, is tantalising. On that spring morning I was particularly taken by boxes of small spiky artichokes, the sort that are best eaten raw in a salad (they apparently grow wild in the mountains behind Palermo), and punnets of tiny wild strawberries.

My next stop was at Palermo's other famous market, the Ballarò. This is much larger than the Vucciria, stretching for about a kilometre along a number of streets in a residential area. Again I found the vegetable stalls ablaze with colour. Eggplants, artichokes, tomatoes, baby broad beans, asparagus and new-season potatoes were heaped on display. At the fish stalls, huge tuna were being sliced into great red steaks on marble slabs. Smaller fish, like sardines and anchovies, surrounded them and there were piles of mussels and sea urchins. I was tempted by cheese stalls selling the full range of Sicilian cheeses, from seasoned hard cheeses such as pecorino to soft and fresh ricottas. There were barrels of olives and bunches of wild fennel, a local favourite. The market was crowded, noisy and full of life. It is easy to see why the Ballarò is considered a great market.

What you don't see at either of these markets is much food being sold ready to eat, which is surprising because Palermo has a very strong tradition of street food. But nevertheless, after all this food viewing your appetite is likely to be aroused. That morning was no exception, so I decided to head to lunch at my favourite restaurant in Palermo, Piccolo Napoli, which is located on a small square near the port.

If I had to generalise, I would say the best food in Sicily comes from the sea. As the local saying goes, 'Il pesce fresco e re di tavola', a fresh fish is king of the table. Piccolo Napoli is a family-owned seafood restaurant, with three generations all working there, from grandmother Corona, to sons Giovanni and Pippo, and grandson Davide. For our late lunch we enjoyed house specialties like pasta con ricci (pasta with fresh sea-urchin roe), gathered by the restaurant's very own

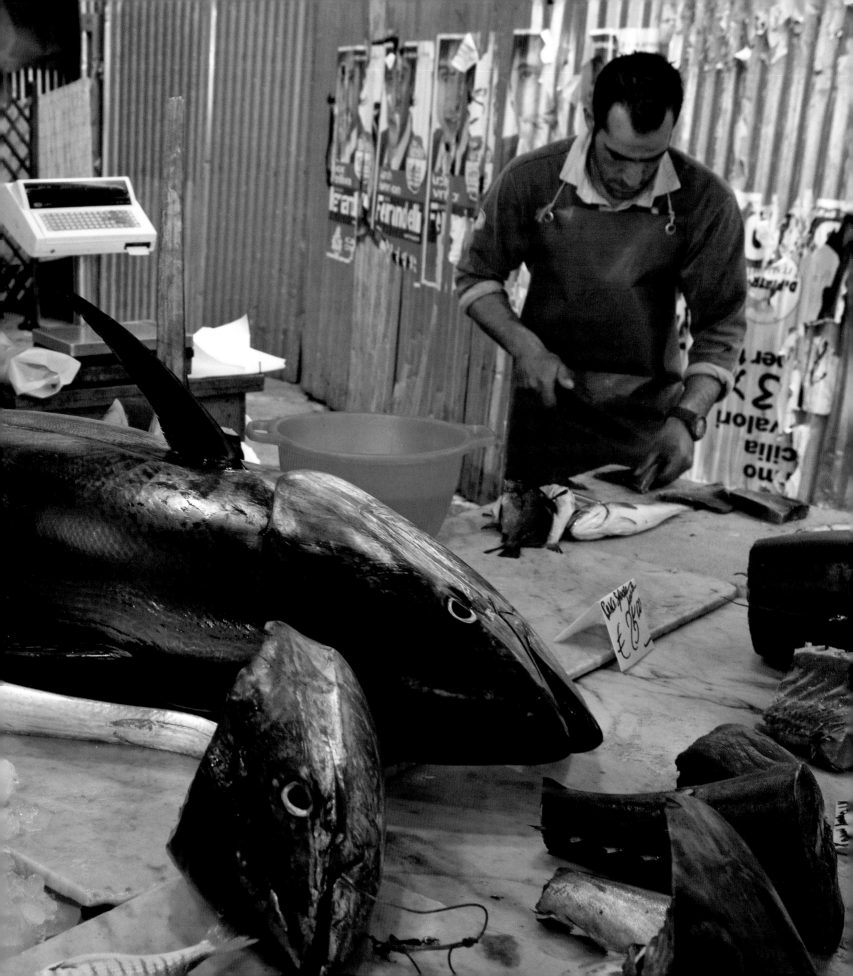

sea-urchin diver; pasta con inchiostro nero (pasta with black squid ink) and involtini di pesce spada (rolled swordfish). The food was served with a local white wine, and followed by Corona's strong espresso coffee. (Sicilian coffee is generally just a finger-width deep in the bottom of a small cup.) This was restaurant food as I like it, with the best ingredients, simply prepared with great care and pride, by people whose business is also their passion.

The next day I was able to experience another side of life in Palermo – home cooking. I had an introduction to Natalia Jung who lives in the seaside town of Mondello, just outside Palermo. Mondello is sited on a big beautiful bay with a crescent of white sand. At one end are stone buildings and a small fishing port. At the other is a mountainous headland. All along the beach there are brightly-coloured bathing cabins and in the middle there is an old 'wedding cake' of a building, a nineteenth-century casino built out on the water.

Natalia lives a little back from the beach in a house that is full of colour to match her vivid personality. We started the day as acquaintances and finished it friends for life. As I watched she cooked two classic Sicilian dishes, a timballo (baked pasta) and

Above: Lunching at
Piccolo Napoli; Nonna
Corona at the coffee
machine (left)
Opposite: At the
Ballarò market

a gelo di anguria (watermelon jelly). They were delicious and we ate them in the way they deserved, in her courtyard garden under a small pergola.

The street-food tradition is very much alive in Palermo and you see very few modern fast-food outlets. Traditionally, the rich Sicilians ate in their palazzi and the poor, who were almost everyone else, ate at street stalls. Food had to be very cheap and very filling. There were panelle (chickpea fritters), crispeddi (fried dumplings filled with anchovy, cheese and wild fennel) and arancine (fried rice balls with cheese filling). There were other fried foods using dough and the cheapest cuts of meat – the unmentionables of the animal, like spleen or intestines. Many of these meat-based offerings are not to my taste, but the others, if done with a light touch, can be a delicious snack.

Another tradition in Sicily is to eat your main meal at midday (life stops for lunch), and this meal is often eaten at home. Among the older generation, the view still lingers that if you are not eating at home then your mother or wife is not looking after you properly. Perhaps this is why there are not as many restaurants as you would expect. When you do eat out the food is very distinctly Sicilian, and usually

via Ruggero Settimo, 68 - tel. 091 581158
Cell. 348 9033563 - PALERMO
www.icuochini.it - e-mail: info@icuochini.it

*Above: Street
scenes in Palermo*

showcases their special pasta dishes, great seafood and good local wines. It's all part of a strong tradition that is a pleasure to experience.

To give you a flavour for life in Palermo, I've begun with a recipe for Arancine. The basic recipe is filled with cheese, and I've added another variation that is made using squid ink.

There are also two vegetable dishes inspired by my visit to the markets – Pomodori Ripieni (stuffed tomatoes) and Finocchio al Forno (baked fennel). I had to include a seafood dish, and by a happy coincidence, the season for swordfish, one of the luxury foods of Sicily, is the spring. And what could be better than Involtini di Pesce Spada (stuffed swordfish rolls)? In this recipe they are stuffed with a mixture that has very traditional ingredients and flavours, such as anchovies, pine nuts and currants.

And, thanks to Natalia, I am delighted to include her classic Palermitano recipes of Timballo and Gelo di Anguria.

Involtini
DI PESCE *Spada*
ROLLED SWORDFISH

12 very thin, small slices of swordfish, each around 12 cm (5 in) square

10 fresh bay leaves

2 tablespoons virgin olive oil

juice of 1 organic lemon

salt flakes

STUFFING

2–3 tablespoons virgin olive oil

1 Spanish onion, finely sliced

2 garlic cloves, crushed

12 anchovy fillets

1 small red chilli, finely sliced

1 bunch Italian flat-leaf parsley, finely chopped

3 tablespoons fresh breadcrumbs

1 tablespoon currants

2 tablespoons pine nuts, lightly toasted

salt and pepper

Preheat the oven to 180°C (350°F).

To make the stuffing, heat the olive oil in a frying pan, then add the onion, garlic, anchovies, chilli and parsley and fry gently for a few minutes. Add the rest of the ingredients and mix well, then remove from the heat.

Put a tablespoon of stuffing on each slice of swordfish. Roll it up very tightly and secure with a toothpick.

Butter a baking dish just large enough to fit the involtini, and arrange them side by side, tucking in a bay leaf here and there between them. Drizzle on the olive oil and bake for 20 minutes. Pour on the lemon juice and season with salt flakes just before serving warm or at room temperature.

Variation

You can also spear the involtini on a skewer, brush them with a little olive oil and cook them on a grill or barbecue.

Serves 6

Arancine

SAVOURY RICE BALLS

300 g (10½ oz) leftover risotto

1 large fresh mozzarella ball, cut into small cubes

2 thick slices of cooked ham, very finely chopped

120 g (4 oz) unbleached plain flour

2 organic eggs, lightly beaten

240 g (9 oz) fresh breadcrumbs

500 ml (17 fl oz) sunflower oil for frying

Traditional Sicilian arancine are filled with a mixture of minced meat, pine nuts, currants, cinnamon and tomato concentrate. This recipe comes from my aunt (who lived in Palermo, but originated from Lugano in Switzerland). She made her arancine with a mozzarella and ham filling; I suppose it was a fusion of north and south.

This dish is best made with leftover risotto. Use Arborio rice as it sticks together better than Carnaroli.

Moisten your hands with a little water, then take a tablespoon of risotto and flatten it gently in the palm of one hand. Place a cube of mozzarella and a little ham in the centre, then shape the risotto around the filling, forming it into a neat, tight ball. Add a little more risotto to cover the filling if necessary.

Roll the arancine in the flour, shaking off any excess. Dip them into the eggs, then coat with breadcrumbs. Pat the arancine well with your hands to make sure they are nice and firm and evenly coated. Place them on a board, ready for frying.

Heat the oil in a medium saucepan. Deep-fry the arancine in batches over a medium–high heat until golden, turning them frequently as they cook. Drain on kitchen paper and keep them warm while you cook the remainder. Serve straight away.

Variation

To make black squid ink arancine, use risotto made with fish stock — you could use leftover fish stock from Fish Couscous (page 97). Add a little squid ink to the risotto to make it black. Follow the method for the arancine recipe above, substituting prawns (shrimp) for the ham.

Makes 15–20 arancine

POMODORI *Ripieni*

STUFFED TOMATOES

8 firm, ripe,
medium-sized tomatoes

50 g (2 oz) unsalted butter

60 ml (2 fl oz) virgin olive oil

1 medium Spanish
onion, very finely diced

10 anchovy fillets in oil,
drained and chopped

2 tablespoons capers in brine,
drained and chopped

2 handfuls Italian flat-leaf
parsley, chopped

75 g (2½ oz) fresh breadcrumbs

50 g (2 oz) pine nuts, toasted

2 handfuls fresh
basil leaves, chopped

salt and pepper

Preheat the oven to 160°C (320°F).

With a sharp knife, slice the tops off the tomatoes. If you like, you can reserve the tops to put back on the tomatoes before baking. Use a small spoon to scoop out just the seeds, leaving the fleshy internal chambers intact. Arrange the tomatoes upside down on a rack and leave to drain for about 30 minutes. Meanwhile, melt the butter and half the oil in a large frying pan. Add the onion and fry gently until soft. Add the anchovies, capers and parsley and cook them for just a few minutes. Add the remaining oil and the breadcrumbs and fry gently for a few minutes more, taking care not to burn the breadcrumbs. Add the pine nuts and basil, and season with a little salt and pepper. Stuff the mixture into the tomatoes, making sure you press it gently into all the internal chambers. Replace the tomato 'lids', if using, then arrange the tomatoes on an oven tray and bake for around an hour.

The tomatoes can be eaten hot or cold.

Serves 4

Finocchio  al Forno

BAKED FENNEL

120 ml (4 fl oz) virgin olive oil

6 fennel bulbs, quartered
(I prefer the long, thin,
male fennel bulbs)

2 Spanish onions, quartered

salt and pepper to taste

1 bunch Italian flat-leaf parsley,
finely chopped

This is a delicious accompaniment to meat or fish dishes.

Preheat the oven to 200°C (400°F).

Drizzle 2 tablespoons of the olive oil over the base of
an ovenproof dish. Scatter in the fennel and onion, then
add the rest of the oil and mix so that the vegetables are
thoroughly coated.

Bake for about 20 minutes, shaking the dish from time to time
to stop the vegetables from sticking to the bottom of the dish.
They should start to colour lightly.

Remove from the oven, season lightly with salt and pepper
and stir in the parsley.

Variation

*I sometimes like to sprinkle on 3 tablespoons of fresh breadcrumbs
and 4 tablespoons of freshly grated Parmigiano before baking in
the oven.*

Serves 4

Timballo DI *Natalia*

NATALIA'S TIMBALLO

TOMATO SAUCE

25 g (1 oz) unsalted butter

2 tablespoons virgin olive oil

1 Spanish onion,
very finely sliced

2 garlic cloves,
very finely sliced

6 fresh sage leaves

2 fresh rosemary sprigs,
woody stalks discarded

2 fresh bay leaves

150 g (5 oz) tomato concentrate

400 g (14 oz) canned
Italian tomatoes

salt and pepper

500 ml (17 fl oz)
sunflower oil for frying

1 medium eggplant,
cut into small cubes

500 g (18 oz) anelli pasta
(or other small pasta
shapes of your choice)

2 tablespoons fresh
breadcrumbs

1 large fresh mozzarella ball,
cut into small cubes

For her timballo, Natalia used a special pasta called anelli that is shaped like little rings. As anelli pasta is only available in Sicily, you can use any small pasta you like, such as farfalline, pennette etc.

Preheat the oven to 200°C (400°F).

To make the sauce, heat the butter and oil in a large frying pan and gently fry the onion, garlic and herbs, taking care not to burn the garlic. When soft, add the tomato concentrate and cook for a few minutes, until the mixture darkens in colour. Stir in the tomatoes and cook over gentle heat for about 20 minutes. Discard the bay leaves and season to your liking.

Heat the sunflower oil in a small frying pan and, when hot, fry the eggplant in batches until pale gold. Remove from the oil and drain on kitchen paper.

Cook the pasta in plenty of boiling salted water until just al dente. Drain well and mix in the tomato sauce so that the pasta is evenly coated.

Thoroughly butter a round non-stick oven dish (25 cm (10 in) diameter and at least 8 cm (3 in) deep). Sprinkle the breadcrumbs over the bottom and up the sides of the dish, then pour in half the pasta. Top with a layer of the eggplant and mozzarella, then cover with the remaining pasta. Bake for 15–20 minutes.

Remove from the oven and leave the timballo to stand for about 3 minutes before turning upside down on a serving dish.

Serves 6

Gelo

DI *Anguria*

WATERMELON JELLY

2 kg (4 lb 6 oz) ripe watermelon

120 g (4 oz) caster
(superfine) sugar

50 g (2 oz) cornflour
(cornstarch)

1 tablespoon jasmine
water (see Note)
(or 1 teaspoon rose water)

1 teaspoon ground cinnamon

50 g (2 oz) dark
chocolate, grated

50 g (2 oz) unsalted pistachio
nuts, finely chopped

jasmine flowers or rose petals
to garnish (optional)

*When Natalia prepared this gelo, she decorated it with chopped
pistachio nuts and grated chocolate, which looked beautiful against
the watermelon pink.*

Slice the watermelon flesh away from the skin and remove all
the pips. Blend in a liquidiser to a smooth purée. A 2 kg (4 lb
6 oz) watermelon should yield around 1 litre (2 pints) of
watermelon purée.

Mix the sugar, cornflour and jasmine water (or rose water)
with a little of the watermelon purée to make a smooth paste.
Stir in the remaining watermelon purée and tip the mixture
into a saucepan. Bring to the boil slowly over a gentle heat.
The mixture will start to thicken. When it does, remove
the pan from the heat and stir in the cinnamon.

Pour the gelo into individual small moulds or one large mould,
which you have moistened with a little water. Leave to set in the
refrigerator for several hours or, better still, overnight.

To serve, loosen the gelo by dunking the mould in warm water
for a few seconds. Invert onto a serving platter and decorate with
chocolate, chopped nuts and jasmine flowers or rose petals.

Note

*To make jasmine water, soak 10 fresh jasmine flowers overnight in
60 ml (2 fl oz) water. The next day, strain the water and use within
24 hours.*

Serves 6

Palermo
OF THE *Gattopardo*

AS YOU WALK THE STREETS OF OLD PALERMO, EVERY NOW AND THEN YOU WILL see a large wooden door set into the high city walls. The door will have elaborate moulding, and above it, in an extravagant flourish of the stonemason's art, a large coat of arms. Likely as not, behind this door will be the palazzo of one of the old noble Sicilian families. Sometimes the facade may be plain, sometimes quite imposing, but however impressive the exterior, it will be nothing compared to the baroque riches inside. In the past, the aristocracy of Sicily owned three-quarters of the arable land but preferred not to live in the country. Instead they congregated in Palermo, built their grand palazzi and seemed to compete with each other as to who could create the most lavish interiors.

This is the Palermo of the Gattopardo (the Leopard), which is so vividly described in the great book of that name by Giuseppe Tomasi, the Prince of Lampedusa. He grew up in that world, only to see it shattered when the Palazzo Lampedusa was destroyed by bombing in World War II. In the 1960s, *The Leopard* was made into a film by Lucchino Visconti (the son of a family who were Dukes of Milan) and it starred Burt Lancaster, Claudia Cardinale and Alain Delon. There is a famous scene

Opposite: Interior of Palazzo Conte Federico

in the movie, lasting about 40 minutes, of a ball for Palermo high society held in a spectacular mirrored ballroom. That room is in the Palazzo Gangi and is still occasionally used today for grand occasions.

Many of these grand palazzi have seen better days. Some are in ruins, some have been taken over by the State or the local government, but some are still owned and cared for by the descendants of the original families. I was able to visit one of these, the Palazzo Conte Federico, which is still used by the Conte, the Contessa and their two sons. The Conte comes from an ancient family who claim descent from a favourite illegitimate son of Frederick Barbarossa, a king of Sicily in the thirteenth century. Frederick, a great character in his day, liked to be called 'Stupor Mundi' (Wonder of the World).

We entered the Palazzo Conte Federico from a narrow street, passing through one of those large wooden doors. After climbing a broad flight of stairs, another wooden door on a small landing opened onto a different world inside.

The Conte himself showed us through the palazzo, opening big shutters as we progressed through the building. We passed through a series of state rooms that

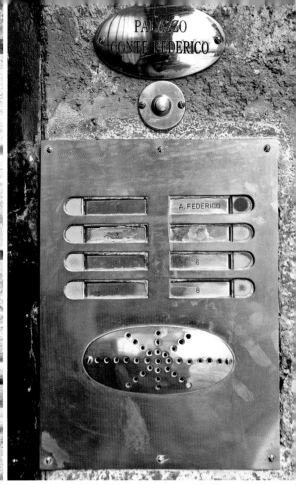

opened one into the other, through generous double doors. The floors were tiled, sometimes in elaborate painted patterns, sometimes in plain terracotta. The walls in the main rooms were lined in silk damask, of pale jade green, strong blue or old gold and many of the vaulted ceilings were elaborately gilded and frescoed. Suspended from their heights were chandeliers in Venetian glass that hung down low into the rooms. We realised that it was impossible to see through all the rooms, from one end of the house to the other, partly because it was such a long distance, and partly because the palazzo itself was shaped in a very shallow curve, following the footings of the old city wall.

Like many European aristocrats, Conte Federico needs to put his inheritance to work to pay for its upkeep, so the state rooms of the palazzo are available to hire for special occasions. But despite the grandeur, it is still a house that is used and very much cared for by the original family. In one room we noted the Contessa's desk set up in a corner. Family photos decorated the walls, together with pictures of the Contessa in her youth as a swimming champion. Another grand room was named after Garibaldi, who was a family friend and whose portrait adorned the wall. There

Above: Entrance to the Palazzo Conte Federico Following pages: Elegant rooms at the Palazzo Conte Federico

*Above: Conte
Federico and his study
Opposite: In the old
kitchen of the palazzo*

we noticed a large cabinet full of the Contessa's swimming trophies and the Conte's trophies from his years racing vintage cars. Set off this room was the Conte's study, tiny by comparison, with just enough room for a desk and chair. Here the walls were lined with books and photos, many showing him with a 'who's who' of the greats of Italian motor racing. Others showed him behind the wheel of his car in famous racing events such as Sicily's Targa Florio. And in another nearby room, full of suits of armour and hanging banners, was a pile of tyres for his 1928 Fiat.

Elsewhere, in the oldest part of the house, we were shown through a medieval tower that housed a large dining area and the kitchen. The Conte explained that kitchens were originally built high off the ground to minimise damage if a fire broke out.

After two hours enjoying the splendours of the Palazzo Conte Federico we thanked the Conte and reluctantly said goodbye, but not before he had recommended his favourite fish restaurant (which we later visited) on the coast out beyond Mondello.

That evening we decided to continue exploring the Palermo of the Gattopardo and booked to go to the opera at the Palermo Opera House, the Teatro Massimo. Anyone who has seen *The Godfather III* movie will recognise the Teatro Massimo as

the setting for the opera performance where the Godfather's daughter is gunned down on the steps outside in a climactic final scene.

We had some time before the evening's performance, so we wandered through the nearby narrow streets and squares drinking aperitivi and nibbling on street food such as panelle and croque. We discovered that this neighborhood was where the local inhabitants came for a less grand form of entertainment. Instead of the opera, you can see puppet shows telling the legends of Sicilian history.

Inside the Teatro Massimo all is crimson and gold. Tier upon tier of private boxes, each with its own small sitting room, rise up on all sides of the auditorium. The corridors are tiled in pale marble, the attendants dressed in long navy-blue coats with crimson collars. As we looked around, it seemed as if the performance of Don Pasquale on the stage was reflected in the theatre of Palermo society.

The following day we returned to the Teatro Massimo to indulge a different appetite. Behind the opera house is the famous Pasticceria Amato, a modest shop-front with a large kitchen where everything is made by hand in the traditional way. Cannoli as thin as cigarettes are a house specialty and they are stored in replicas of

*Above: Puppets from
the local puppet theatre
Opposite: Teatro
Massimo*

Above: Delicacies from Pasticceria Amato

pretty nineteenth-century boxes, lined with silver paper, where they stay fresh for forty-eight hours. Other delights are brioches filled with house-made ice cream (a typical Sicilian alternative to the wafer cone), tiny pastries filled with ricotta and dusted with pistachio nuts, and boxes of exotic marzipan fruits. The proprietors, Pina and Franco Boscanno, both work there, he in the kitchen and she behind the counter. The Pasticceria Amato is a beautiful survivor of old Palermo.

Although its golden age was from the tenth to the twelfth centuries, Palermo had a renaissance in the second half of the nineteenth century. A new grand avenue, the Viale della Liberta, was built west of the city and some of the old Sicilian families and the 'new rich' built palazzi there, many in beautiful gardens with a range of exotic trees and shrubs. Palermo became one of the fashionable cities of Europe and visitors such as the future King Edward VII, the Kaiser of Germany and the Dowager Empress of Russia arrived there on their yachts. Today much of this grandeur has disappeared, replaced by anonymous tower blocks built in the 1970s when it seemed as if anyone could build anything they liked, anywhere. As Sicilians say, 'Come era bella una volta,' (Once upon a time it was really beautiful).

Dining in these grand houses would have been a fairly elaborate experience. It was fashionable to have French chefs known as Monzù, a Sicilian corruption of 'Monsieur'. The Monzù prepared what we would call international cuisine; the local food of the poor was considered entirely unsuitable. Occasionally a traditional dish, such as timballo, would be re-created and refined to be served at the best tables. Here is the description of a timballo from *The Leopard*:

> *The burnished gold of the crusts, the fragrance of sugar and cinnamon they exuded, were but preludes to the delights released from the interior when the knife broke the crust; first came a spice-laden haze, then chicken livers, hard-boiled eggs, sliced ham, chicken and truffles in masses of piping-hot, glistening macaroni to which the meat juice gave an exquisite hue of suede.*

Clearly the Prince of Lampedusa was what they call in Sicily 'una bella forchetta', literally 'a good fork' but meaning someone who likes his food!

With the decline of the noble houses, the Monzù often left to establish Palermo's first good restaurants. They began to use more local ingredients and recipes, albeit

Above: Rolling cornetti in the kitchen at Pasticceria Amato

with some refinement. In this way the cooking of the noble houses joined with 'cucina povera' to produce the dishes that you find today.

The recipes I have selected for this chapter are what I imagine the Monzù might serve, not so much in the grand houses – which would be too elaborate for the way we live today – but in their own restaurants.

Fritella is a marvellous mixed vegetable dish, which is good on its own as a light meal or served as an accompaniment to fish or meat. Insalata Pantesca is a salad made with potatoes, capers, olives, onions and tomatoes; it looks colourful and tastes like a hot spring day.

Sarde Beccafico takes the humble sardine to a new level of refinement by stuffing it with Moorish-influenced ingredients and rolling it up to form little parcels. Involtini con Carciofi are veal rolls stuffed with artichokes.

The final recipe is for one of Sicily's most famous dishes, Cassata. The local version is a ricotta-based cake, not an ice cream, and it is always elaborately decorated with marzipan icing and covered in frills and fancies. In Palermo if you want to say that a woman is really beautiful you say she is 'bella come una cassata' – as beautiful as a cassata.

Above: Street scenes, Palermo
Opposite: The Botanic Gardens, Palermo

Frittella

YOUNG BROAD BEANS,
ARTICHOKES AND PEAS

3–4 artichokes

juice of 2 organic lemons,
mixed with 1 litre water

80 ml (3 fl oz)
extra-virgin olive oil

50 g (2 oz) unsalted butter

20 shallots, finely sliced

400 g (14 oz) podded
fresh broad beans,
blanched and peeled

400 g (14 oz) podded fresh peas

salt and pepper

½ bunch Italian flat-leaf
parsley, finely chopped

2 wild fennel sprigs,
finely chopped

This dish can be served as a light starter or as an accompaniment to meat dishes such as Involtini con Carciofi (page 50).

To prepare the artichokes, remove the tough outer leaves and the choke and slice a third off the tops. Slice them into thin wedges and quickly place them in the lemon water to stop the flesh discolouring.

Remove the artichokes from the lemon water and dry them thoroughly on kitchen paper. Heat 2 tablespoons of the oil and all the butter in a frying pan. Add the artichokes and shallots and cook gently for a few minutes.

Add 125 ml (4 fl oz) water to the pan. Stir in the broad beans and peas and cook until they are just tender, about 8 minutes. Season with salt and pepper and stir in the herbs and the remaining olive oil. Serve at room temperature.

Serves 4

Insalata *Pantesca*

POTATO AND TOMATO SALAD

4 medium-sized potatoes,
boiled, peeled and sliced

1 small Spanish onion,
very thinly sliced

8 ripe tomatoes, diced

12 black or green olives, pitted

30 g (1 oz) capers in brine,
drained and chopped

1 handful fresh basil leaves

1 handful fresh oregano leaves

80 ml (3 fl oz) virgin olive oil

salt and pepper

This tasty salad makes a lovely light starter. You can easily turn it into a light meal by adding a can of good-quality tuna, well drained of its oil.

Toss all the ingredients together gently but thoroughly, and serve with plenty of crusty bread.

Serves 4

Sarde Beccafico

STUFFED SARDINES,
BECCAFICO STYLE

700 g (1 lb 8 oz) fresh sardines

15 fresh bay leaves

handful each of chopped
Italian flat-leaf parsley
and mint to serve

STUFFING

120–200 ml (4–7 fl oz)
virgin olive oil

5 anchovy fillets

100 g (3½ oz) fresh
breadcrumbs

2 tablespoons finely chopped
Italian flat-leaf parsley

1 tablespoon capers in brine,
drained and finely chopped
(optional)

3 tablespoons currants

4 tablespoons pine nuts, toasted

grated zest and juice of
1 organic lemon

1 teaspoon sugar

salt and pepper

This is the perfect dish to prepare in springtime, when the sardines are plump and tender.

Preheat the oven to 200°C (400°F).

Scrape away the scales from the sardines. Pull the heads away from the bodies – the backbone will naturally come away too – making sure the tail stays attached to the two fillets. Rinse them well then dry them on kitchen paper.

To make the stuffing, heat half the olive oil in a small frying pan, then add the anchovies and let them melt, stirring continuously for about a minute. Add the breadcrumbs and cook for another minute then add the parsley, mix well and take off the heat.

Stir in the capers, currants, pine nuts, lemon zest (reserving the juice for later), sugar and a little salt and pepper.

Open out the sardines and lay them out flat on a work surface. Place a teaspoon of the stuffing mixture onto each fish, arranging it neatly along its length. Lift the sides of the fish up to enclose the stuffing and secure with 2 toothpicks.

Butter an ovenproof dish, around 18 x 30 cm (7½ x 12 in). Arrange the stuffed sardines in the dish, packing them in tightly to prevent them opening up. Tuck the bay leaves in between the sardines and sprinkle on any leftover stuffing mixture. Drizzle over the remaining oil and bake for 15 minutes until golden brown. Remove from the oven and pour on the reserved lemon juice. Add the fresh herbs just before serving. You can serve this dish hot or cold, although I like it best at room temperature.

Serves 4

Involtini
CON *Carciofi*

ROLLED VEAL WITH ARTICHOKES

600 g (1 lb 5 oz) veal
backstraps (loins)

80 g (3 oz) Italian
prosciutto, finely diced

90 g (3 oz) unsalted butter at
room temperature

juice of ½ organic lemon

2 artichokes

60 g (2 oz) unbleached
plain flour

80 ml (3 fl oz) virgin olive oil

fresh sage leaves

150 ml (5 fl oz) dry white wine

salt and pepper

*I like to serve these involtini with Potato and Leek Gratin
(page 186).*

Cut the veal into 8 thin slices and pat dry with kitchen paper.

Mix the prosciutto into the softened butter.

Bring a saucepan of salted water to the boil, then add the lemon
juice. To prepare the artichokes, trim the stalks away and remove
the tough outer leaves, then slice a third off the tops. Add them
to the boiling water and cook for 2 minutes. Remove from the
water and drain upside down on a rack. When cool enough to
handle, cut each artichoke into 8 slices, removing hairy bits of
choke as necessary.

Spread each slice of veal with a little of the butter mixture and
top with 2 slices of artichoke. Roll the meat up tightly and secure
with a toothpick or string.

Roll the involtini in the flour.

Heat the olive oil in a large frying pan then add the sage leaves
and involtini. Turn them around in the oil so that they brown
evenly all over. Add the wine and stir well, making sure you
scrape up all the tasty bits from the bottom of the pan. Season
with salt and pepper then cover the pan and simmer over a very
low heat for 10–15 minutes. Add a little more wine if need be.

Serves 4

Cassata *Siciliana*

MARIA'S SPONGE CAKE

3 organic eggs

120 g (4 oz) caster
(superfine) sugar

150 g (5 oz) self-raising flour

1 teaspoon baking powder

pinch of salt

grated zest of 1 organic lemon

2 tablespoons hot water

RICOTTA FILLING

800 g (1 lb 11 oz) fresh ricotta

300 g (10½ oz) caster
(superfine) sugar

3 tablespoons good Marsala

100 g (3½ oz) dark chocolate,
chopped into little pieces

100 g (3½ oz) candied
fruit, optional

MARZIPAN

200 g (7 oz) ground almonds

200 g (7 oz) icing
(confectioner's) sugar

2 teaspoons orange-blossom
water or rose water

1 drop green food colouring

around 50 ml (2 fl oz) water

GARNISH

candied fruit, optional

melted dark or
white chocolate, optional

Preheat the oven to 180ºC (350ºF). Line a 30 x 20 cm (12 x 8 in) rectangular cake tin with greaseproof paper then butter the paper generously.

To make the sponge, beat the eggs until light and fluffy then, still beating, gradually add the sugar. Slowly mix in the flour, baking powder, salt and lemon zest, followed by the water. Pour the mixture into the prepared cake tin. Cook for about 8 minutes, or until firm to the touch.

Remove from the oven and leave to cool in the tin for a few minutes before turning onto a cake rack. When cold, carefully cut the sponge horizontally through the centre, creating 2 thin slices. Then cut out 2 x 21 cm (8¼ in) circles and cut the rest of the sponge into wide strips.

Line the base and sides of a 22 cm (9 in) springform cake tin with greaseproof paper. Arrange one sponge circle in the bottom of the cake tin and neatly line the sides with the strips of cake so there are no gaps.

To make the ricotta filling, beat the ricotta with the sugar and Marsala until smooth. Fold in the chocolate and candied fruit, if using. Spoon the filling into the sponge-lined cake tin. Place the remaining sponge circle on top and press gently. Transfer to the refrigerator for a few hours or, better still, overnight.

To make the marzipan, combine the ground almonds, icing sugar, flower water and food colouring with just enough water to form a stiff paste. Roll out the marzipan to 1 cm thickness. Turn the cassata out onto a serving plate and cover with marzipan. Decorate with more candied fruit or patterns in melted chocolate.

Serves 6

The Tuna Coast

FOR CENTURIES THE NORTHWEST COAST OF SICILY HAS BEEN THE SITE OF AN
extraordinary natural phenomenon. Sometime around the end of May and early
June, large schools of tuna arrive from the Atlantic and move to their spawn-
ing grounds in the Mediterranean. As they migrate the fish pass close by the Egadi
Islands and then move in towards the Sicilian coastline as they head towards Palermo
and the waters beyond.

It is easy to imagine that for as long as men on the land have been watching the
tuna they must have been consumed by dreams of catching them. At first, small
boats would have been launched from the beaches and ports along the coast and
fishing lines would have been thrown into the waters. Then, with the arrival of
the Moors, a new technique was introduced that greatly increased the size of the
catch and spawned a whole industry. Huge nets were laid at sea, anchored to the
bottom and arranged in an elaborate pattern of wings to tunnel the migrating fish
towards a central point. At the moment the head fisherman (who are still known
by the Moorish name 'ras') judged right, the nets were closed, trapping the fish in
one small area. There the 'mattanza', a mass ritual of catching and killing the tuna,

*Opposite: The Kursaal
Tonnara on the
Palermo coast*

55

*Above: A tonnara fishing
base near Palermo
Opposite: Tonnara
at Mondello*

would take place. For hundreds of years now, the mattanza has been one of the great annual events of life on this coast.

The northwest coast of Sicily is dotted with distinctive stone buildings and towers called 'tonnare', fishing bases that used to service the mattanza. Traditionally, these would include a boat shed to store the long wooden rowing boats and nets, a factory area where the fish would be processed and a watchtower to alert the fishermen when the tuna were arriving. Along this part of the coast one tower would always be in sight of the next, so signals could be exchanged. Many also served to warn against marauding pirates from the Barbary Coast of North Africa.

Although tonnare can be seen all along the northwest coast, the main focus of the mattanza has always been at Favignana in the Egadi Islands and at Trapani on the northwest coast of Sicily. These are the places where the tuna first touch the coast on their migration. In the early nineteenth century, the first cannery was established on Favignana and tuna from Sicily was exported to the world. Just south of Trapani there are extensive salt pans. Historically the availability of salt was important as it meant the tuna could be preserved and sold for an extended season, not just fresh.

We visited the island of Favignana on a lovely spring morning – it is a place almost entirely dedicated to tuna fishing. At the port we admired the old boat sheds and the factory of a huge tonnara. This, we learnt, was the enterprise of the local Florio family, who started the canning industry there during the nineteenth century. Their house near the port, the gothic Villa Florio, is in the process of being restored. In the town itself we found many shops dedicated to tuna produce, where they sold everything from tinned tuna and smoked tuna to salted tuna and tuna in oil. We even spotted tuna roe that had been dried to become the famous bottarga. We discovered that there is a difference between tuna caught in the mattanza and tuna caught 'volante' (out of season). And naturally, the mattanza tuna is greatly preferred. We were told that the best part of the tuna is the flesh around the stomach. The fishermen are in Favignana in force too. The town squares are full of men with the weather-beaten faces of old seafarers. Tuna may not be caught in great quantities anymore, but on Favignana the traditions are being preserved.

On the ferry journey back to Trapani we noticed an unusual site to the south of the city – the profiles of windmills, their sails turning in the sea breeze. These

working windmills are close to the old salt pans, which are still in production today. The salt pans are on the edge of a shallow lagoon between the island of Mozia, an old Carthaginian settlement, and the mainland. An elaborate system of levies and sluices controls the flooding of the bays, where the sea water is left until it evaporates over the summer months. Today the salt is no longer used to preserve the tuna catch, but is sold as a gourmet natural product.

To arrive at the busy port of Trapani by sea is to get the real flavour of the city. Ferries and working boats depart for the Egadi Islands and Pantelleria to the west, as well as to Sardinia in the north and to the coast of Africa to the south. Trapani itself has something of a North African feel about it. It might be because of the Moorish influence and the pale, bleached-sand colour of its stone buildings; perhaps it's because of the signs on the breakwater announcing the departure of ferries to Tunisia. The Moorish influence is also found in the local food. We were excited to learn that the specialty of Trapani is couscous, grains of semolina made from hard durum wheat, which are steamed over an aromatic broth. In North Africa couscous is accompanied by meat (lamb or goat) but in Trapani it is served with fish.

Above and opposite:
The port at Favignana;
the long mattanza boats
(top left)

That evening we ate at Ai Lumi, a restaurant and wine bar on the main street. The wines were exceptional, with the first three pages of the wine list devoted to local wines – all available by the glass. The nearby wine-growing areas are on the flat valleys inland from the sea. White wines are grown on the low country, reds on the slopes above, and we were delighted to sample a selection of both. Naturally we also tried a few of their tuna dishes. One of my favourites, tonno ammarinato, was particularly memorable and was made with onions cooked in vinegar. At the end of dinner we tried two digestivi, just to settle the stomach. The first came from the nearby town of Marsala. It was not technically a Marsala wine because its alcohol content was too low (19.5 per cent rather than 20 per cent), but was made by the same process. It was dry and aromatic and absolutely perfect with a very sweet dessert like cassata. We also tasted Passito, a sweet wine made from the zibibbo grapes that are grown on the island of Pantelleria off the west coast. It was luscious and raisiny, and made a great accompaniment to ricotta cake.

Although tuna fishing and the tuna industry still dominate this part of Sicily, the tuna catch is a fraction of what it used to be, mostly because the fish are now

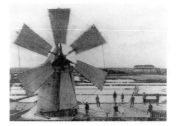

Opposite: Windmills at the salt pans, Trapani
Following pages: The tonnara at Scopello; the bay and surrounds

Kursaal Tonnara
VERGINE MARIA

*Above: Claudio and I
enjoy aperitivi at the
Kursaal Tonnara
Opposite: The Kursaal
Tonnara at dusk*

caught by industrial-scale fleets before they reach the port at Favignana. The small
boats still row out to set the nets – I saw this during my visit – and the mattanza
still takes place. But along the rest of the coastline the tonnare have nearly all closed
down. All that remains are the old stone boat sheds and watchtowers in their prime
positions on the waterfront.

We visited one of these the following day on a trip to the small seaside village
of Scopello. It is the site of a magnificent disused tonnara, set on a small bay with
limestone pinnacles rising from the waters and with watchtowers set on the headlands. The slopes behind the bay were covered in flowering broom, cistus, valerian,
Queen Anne's lace, acanthus and giant teasels. We ate a simple fish lunch at a restaurant perched high above the bay surrounded by a large party celebrating the First
Communion of two young boys.

On another evening we drove out from Palermo to visit an old tonnara near the
town of Mondello. The Kursaal Tonnara is owned by Alberto Coppola, who has also
beautifully restored an old building in the city walls of Palermo into a well-known
restaurant and bookshop. Albert is now working the same magic at his tonnara. The

oldest part of the building dates from the fourteenth century, and it was in use up until 1953. The Kursaal Tonnara is situated right on the water and Alberto has created a beautiful garden within the walls and a restaurant with a lovely view of the sea. There we enjoyed his hospitality as the sun set on a late spring evening.

In thinking about dishes from the tuna coast the only difficulty is in deciding which recipes to include. In Sicily tuna is prepared in so many different ways and most of them are delicious. My first choice is Finissima di Tonno, a dish of finely sliced raw tuna that is topped with fried capers. The capers are also a Sicilian specialty and come from the islands of Pantelleria or Salina.

Next, there is a recipe for Pâté di Tonno. You won't find this dish in Trapani — it is my grandfather's creation. He had a famous restaurant in Lugano in southern Switzerland and this is a dish he devised using canned tuna in a period of wartime rationing (although it's exceptional at any time). Although canned tuna has quite a different flavour to fresh tuna, I belive this is something to be embraced not rejected. After all, you wouldn't turn down prosciutto because it doesn't taste like fresh pork! Of course tuna can also be preserved in oil. I have included a recipe for Tonno Sott'Olio using canned tuna.

Two of my other favourites are Tonno al Forno, which is a baked tuna dish, and my version of the Tonno Ammarinato that we tasted at Ai Lumi.

Finally, to finish up there is a Torta di Ornella, made with almonds and lemon, which would be delicious served with a glass of Passito di Pantelleria.

Left: An old photograph of the mattanza
Above: Claudio and Michele admire the view

Finissima

DI Tonno

TUNA CARPACCIO

1 x 25 cm (10 in) square
sheet of good-quality
butter puff pastry

sea salt flakes

6 teaspoons capers
in brine, drained

200–300 ml (7–10 fl oz)
sunflower oil for frying

250–300 g (9–10 oz)
sashimi-grade tuna

extra-virgin olive oil

organic lemon juice

1 small red chilli, very
finely sliced (optional)

*This is the simplest of dishes to make, and is delicious as a light
starter or as part of an antipasto. Ask your fishmonger to slice
the sashimi tuna for you as thinly as possible. Allow 3–4 small
slices per person.*

Preheat the oven to 180°C (350°F).

Cut the pastry sheet into 6 equal rectangles. Score the surface
on the diagonal with a sharp knife, and sprinkle with a few salt
flakes. Bake for 6 minutes, or until golden brown.

Heat the sunflower oil in a small saucepan until hot. Fry the
capers until they turn crisp, then remove from the oil and drain
on kitchen paper.

Just before serving, arrange 3–4 slices of tuna on each pastry
base. Drizzle on a little olive oil and lemon juice, then sprinkle
on the capers and chilli, if using. There is no need to season
further as the capers are salty enough.

Serves 6

Pâté

DI Tonno

TUNA PÂTÉ

400 g (14 oz) canned tuna in oil

200 g (7 oz) unsalted butter, cut into small cubes

3 tablespoons virgin olive oil

1 large Spanish onion, finely chopped

3 cloves garlic, sliced

10 fresh sage leaves

20 anchovy fillets in oil, drained

150 ml (5 fl oz) medium–dry Marsala

1 medium-sized potato, boiled, peeled and diced

salt and freshly ground black pepper

This is a variation on the tuna pâté that my grandfather used to make, which appeared in Under The Olive Tree. *The version below was specially adapted by my mother for large numbers of people. The potato makes the pâté lighter — and makes it go further!*

Drain the tuna and place it in a food processor.

Heat about 50 g (2 oz) of the butter in a frying pan with the olive oil. Add the onion, garlic and sage leaves and fry gently for a few minutes. Add the anchovies and let them melt. Pour in the Marsala and stir until it evaporates. Remove the pan from the heat and add the rest of the butter. Leave it to melt.

Add the potato and the onion mixture to the tuna. Process for about 5 minutes to form a very smooth, pale purée. Taste and adjust the seasoning to your liking, adding more pepper if necessary. Tip into a serving bowl and transfer to the refrigerator until it sets hard.

Serves 6

Tonno

SOTT' *Olio*

TUNA IN OIL

400 g (14 oz) canned
tuna in oil, drained

50 g (2 oz) unsalted pistachio
nuts, toasted and roughly
chopped

25 g (1 oz) capers
in brine, drained

6–8 cornichons in brine,
drained and diced

125 ml (4 fl oz) virgin olive oil

*This is delicious served as a stuzzichino with drinks, or as part
of an antipasto.*

Combine all the ingredients in a mixing bowl and use a fork
to mix them together roughly. I like it to be still a bit chunky.
Serve with crusty sourdough bread.

Serves 4–6

Tonno  al Forno

BAKED TUNA

2 x 300 g (10½ oz) tuna steaks, around 1 cm (½ in) thick

juice of 1 organic lemon

salt flakes

125 ml (4 fl oz) virgin olive oil

110 g (3½ oz) capers in brine, drained and finely chopped

½ bunch Italian flat-leaf parsley, finely chopped

3 cloves garlic, roughly chopped

500 g (1lb 2 oz) waxy potatoes, parboiled, then peeled and coarsely grated

250 g (9 oz) Spanish onions, peeled and coarsely grated

salt and pepper

fresh oregano leaves

Preheat oven to 200°C (400°F).

Pat the tuna steaks dry with kitchen paper and put them in a shallow dish. Sprinkle on 2 tablespoons of the lemon juice and a few salt flakes. Leave to rest for about 15 minutes.

Combine the remaining lemon juice with the oil, capers, parsley and garlic. Add the grated potatoes and onions and fold everything together well with a wooden spoon. Season lightly with a little salt and some pepper.

Lightly oil an ovenproof baking dish, which is just large enough to hold the tuna steaks.

Tip half the potato mixture into the dish. Arrange the tuna steaks on top, then cover with the remaining potato mixture. Bake for 35 minutes until the surface is golden brown. The tuna should be cooked, but still moist.

Sprinkle with the oregano leaves and serve hot from the oven dish.

Serves 4–6

Tonno *Ammarinato*

SWEET AND SOUR TUNA

1 kg (2 lb 3 oz) fresh tuna,
cut into steaks about 2 cm
(½ in) thick

50 g (2 oz) unsalted butter

80 ml (3 fl oz) virgin olive oil

2 large Spanish onions,
finely sliced

1 teaspoon caster
(superfine) sugar

60 ml (2 fl oz) good-quality
red-wine vinegar

1 bunch Italian flat-leaf parsley,
finely chopped

salt and pepper

With a very sharp knife cut the tuna steaks into cubes of
3 x 2 cm (1¼ x ¾ in).

Heat the butter and oil in a large frying pan. Add the onions
and fry over a low heat until soft and translucent. Increase the
heat to medium, add the sugar and cook for a few more minutes.
Push the onions to the edge of the pan and add the tuna. Cook
briefly until the tuna pieces are lightly browned all over. Add
the vinegar and cook until it has evaporated. Carefully stir in the
parsley then remove the pan from the heat. Cover with a lid and
leave to stand for a few minutes so the flavours amalgamate.
Taste and adjust the seasoning to your liking before serving.

Serves 6

Torta *Ornella*

RICOTTA, ALMOND
AND LEMON CAKE

250 g (9 oz) unsalted butter at
room temperature

250 g (9 oz) caster (superfine)
sugar

6 organic eggs, separated

250 g (9 oz) almonds, roasted
then ground

70 g (2½ oz) self-raising flour

pinch of salt

finely grated zest of 5 organic
lemons and juice of 4 lemons

400 g (14 oz) fresh ricotta

Preheat the oven to 180ºC (350ºF). Butter a 25 cm (10 in)
round cake tin.

Beat the butter and sugar in an electric mixer until very light and
fluffy. With the motor running, add the egg yolks, one at a time,
until all are incorporated.

Combine the ground almonds with the flour, salt and lemon zest.
Fold into the batter.

Whisk the lemon juice with the ricotta until light and airy.
Fold into the cake batter.

Beat the egg whites until they form soft peaks. Fold them
carefully into the batter.

Tip the batter into the prepared cake tin and bake for
50 minutes. Test for doneness by inserting a skewer into the
cake. It should come out clean when cooked through.

Remove the cake from the oven and turn it out onto a cake
rack to cool. It will remain nice and moist for a few days.

Serves 6—8

The Fertile West

THE COASTAL PLAINS OF WEST SICILY BETWEEN TRAPANI AND MARSALA ARE bursting with carefully-tended agriculture. Close to the sea there are vineyards and olive groves, while further inland the valleys are full of wheat fields, carob plantations and more vineyards and olive trees. Driving through these valleys in springtime you can understand why Sicily was such a magnet for invaders through the centuries. It is a picture of fertility and fruitfulness.

This area is well-known for its production of olive oil. It has to be said that Sicilian olive oil has had a mixed reputation. In some areas large co-operatives with poor agricultural and oil-making techniques have delivered a very ordinary product. More recently, though, a number of producers have begun to produce exceptional oils, using strict quality control and attention to detail.

One particular olive oil from a farm near Trapani had been judged very highly in blind tasting tests, so I arranged a visit. The oil is called Titone, which is the family name of the father and daughter who own and manage the business. Titone oil is produced organically showing yet again that you should seek out organic produce not only because it is healthy but also because it tastes so good.

Opposite: Vines outside Marsala

"Il cibo è la migliore medicina
La medicina migliore è il cibo"
IPPOCRATE

*Above: At the Titone
olive grove;
Drs Antonella and
Nicola Titone (right)*

The Titone family have been pharmacists in Marsala since 1837 and boast Garibaldi as one of their early clients. The current patriarch, Dr Nicola Titone, and his daughter, Dr Antonella Titone, both trained as pharmacists, and it was their technical knowledge that enabled them to devise ways to organically control pests such as the olive fly in their groves. The Titone's attention to organic quality is apparent everywhere. Neither the olive trees nor the ground around them are sprayed, the fruit is hand-picked at precisely the right moment and the processing area is as meticulous and spick and span as a dairy. The oil itself is blended so that it is broadly similar from year to year. It is green and grassy, slightly sharp with a touch of pepper and a whole noseful of other wonderful aromatics.

We tasted the Titone olive oil in the best possible manner – drizzled onto a fresh crusty loaf of local bread, sprinkled with a little salt (perhaps from the nearby salt pans), and topped with a ripe tomato and a few basil leaves. It was sensational. To finish we each had a cannoli with a light ricotta filling, fresh from the local baker. This simple meal was as memorable as any we had in Sicily.

After lunch we headed down the coast towards Marsala where we had booked to stay at an agriturismo, a rural bed-and-breakfast. You can find these family-run operations all around Sicily. They are usually run as an add-on to the business of farming. When you stay, it is like staying with a family, but because they are farmers there is the added advantage that they can tell you all about the local produce. Although some agriturismi are strictly bed-and-breakfast, many will also cook dinner for you in the evening. Some of the most enjoyable dining we had in Sicily was in agriturismi.

The agriturismo we were staying at was called Baglio Vajarassa, and is run by a local character called Nardino Argate. From our upstairs bedroom we had a view across a field of vines that had been planted so close to the sea that they had to be cut low to avoid salt spray. Beyond them we could see a shallow bay with the island of Mozia in the distance. Off to one side we could see the windmills of the nearby salt pans and behind the two-storey house was a large paved courtyard with shade trees – the ideal spot for drinks and dinner on a hot evening.

Nardino had promised to make me his fish couscous and that is what we ate for dinner. The couscous itself was steamed over fish broth and accompanied by a plate

Above: Street scenes, Marsala

of small fish freshly caught from the bay. With local wine and a glass of Marsala to finish, it was everything that local eating should be.

The following day we drove to the city of Marsala to visit the cellars of Cantina Florio, the largest producer of Marsala wines. The city is surrounded by old walls and is well preserved and cared-for. The sand-coloured stone buildings and streets give it a distinctive character. During our visit we learnt that the city has a distinguished modern history – it is where Garibaldi landed to begin his successful campaign to win Sicily for the new united Italian State. He is celebrated everywhere.

The history of Marsala wine is also fascinating. Like port, sherry and claret, it was a wine developed in a foreign country for the English market. It was actually created by an enterprising English merchant called John Woodhouse, who wanted to fortify the local wine so it would keep when exported. As luck would have it, the British fleet in the Mediterranean, commanded by Admiral Lord Nelson, was deprived of wine from Spain because of the war at the time. So they ordered 500 'pipes' (about 210,000 litres) of Marsala from Woodhouse and the British sailors quickly developed a taste for it.

Lord Nelson, of course, went on to famous victories, a scandalous love affair with Emma Hamilton, the wife of the British Ambassador to the court in Naples, and was eventually rewarded for defeating Napoleon with the Sicilian title of Duke of Bronte and vast estates of land close to Mount Etna.

Another English merchant, Benjamin Ingham, developed techniques for greatly improving the quality of Marsala. The wine became fashionable in England and was eventually sold all around the world. Woodhouse returned to England but Ingham and his nephews and heirs, the Whittakers, went on to make a fortune and built palazzi in Palermo and Rome.

The Woodhouse and Ingham companies subsequently merged with the Sicilian Florio company and have recently been taken over by an international drinks conglomerate. Today the wine is produced at the Cantina Florio, which is situated in a large walled compound on the seafront just outside the city of Marsala. In times of trouble (and there seems to have been a lot of them) the Woodhouses, Inghams, Whittakers and Florios would retreat to their palazzo compounds for safety, waiting out any danger there.

Above: Cantina Florio

Marsala wine is still made by the solera method, following the techniques developed by Ingham. This is the same way sherry is made, which is how Ingham got the idea. A quantity of old wine is used to start fermentation in the barrels of new wine and the famous yeasts live on. The process can be repeated and repeated – in fact the Marsala-style digestivo we enjoyed so much at dinner in Trapani was the result of twenty repetitions.

The cantina, or above-ground cellars, are oriented to get a gentle sea breeze to control temperature. Additional cooling comes from the seawater table, which is just below the hard yellow earth floor. Humidity is seen as important to promote the growth of the moulds and yeasts that mature the wine. In the cantina, rows of huge oak barrels hold the wine as it ages. In the small museum attached to the cantina, the original contract between Nelson and Woodhouse is on display (dated 18 March 1800), together with bottles of Marsala dating back to 1868, the year Garibaldi launched his campaign.

Marsala is commonly thought to be a sweet wine, but like sherry, it can range from very sweet to bone dry. As an aperitivo or a digestivo, I particularly like a fairly

Above: A Marsala tasting

dry Marsala; these tend to be deep amber in colour with lots of interesting aromas. As I found in Trapani, a dry Marsala is also an excellent accompaniment to a very sweet dessert. I often use a medium–sweet Marsala in cooking for a richer taste.

For recipes that remind me of my time in Marsala and the countryside nearby, there is no better place to start than our lunch at the Titone Olive Grove. For Pane Cunzatu (seasoned bread), as it is known locally, all you need is some fresh crusty bread, good olive oil, salt, tomatoes and basil. Bread can be seasoned in many ways but this is probably the classic combination.

I have also included two vegetable dishes, Involtini di Melanzane (rolled eggplant) and Peperonata, made from red and yellow peppers and spiced with the full array of Sicilian ingredients – olives, anchovies, capers, pine nuts, mint, garlic and chilli.

Of course I have to include a recipe for fish couscous. Eating couscous is a bit like eating a fondue – it's a communal activity with a central plate and accompanying dishes that are passed around the table. It is best eaten with a number of people, as conviviality is an important ingredient.

I have also included a rabbit recipe, Coniglio con Mandorle, (rabbit with almonds). Sicilians are not great meat eaters, but you find wild rabbits in these areas and locals enjoy both hunting and eating them.

Perhaps the most famous Sicilian pastries are Cannoli: deep-fried thin pastry tubes that are filled with ricotta. The ricotta is sweetened and can be flavoured with candied fruit or chocolate. One of the nicest versions we found were the ones we ate for lunch at Titone's, and I have included a recipe here.

Coniglio
CON Mandorle
RABBIT WITH ALMONDS

1 large organic rabbit
(or 2 smaller rabbits),
cut into pieces

3 fresh bay leaves

1 fresh rosemary sprig

8 fresh sage leaves

½–1 bottle dry Marsala

unbleached plain flour
for dusting

3 tablespoons virgin olive oil

1 Spanish onion, chopped

4 anchovy fillets in oil, drained

100 g (3½ oz) almonds,
lightly toasted

50 g (2 oz) pine nuts,
lightly toasted

50 g (2 oz) currants

50 g (2 oz) capers

salt and pepper

juice of 1 organic lemon

This dish is delicious served with plain couscous to soak up the wonderful sauce. If you really don't like rabbit, you can use organic chicken pieces instead.

Toss the rabbit pieces in the herbs and place in a shallow dish. Pour on the Marsala and leave to marinate in the refrigerator for 4 hours or, better still, overnight.

Remove the rabbit pieces from the marinade and dust with the flour, shaking off any excess.

Heat the olive oil in a large saucepan just large enough to hold the rabbit pieces snugly. Add the onion and fry gently until soft and translucent. Once the onion starts to colour, add the rabbit pieces and brown all over. Add the marinade, which should nearly cover the rabbit (add some extra Marsala if there is not enough). Cook for a few minutes, scraping up any sticky bits from the bottom of the pan. Add the anchovies, cover the pan and simmer over a very low heat for 25 minutes.

Turn the rabbit pieces in the sauce, adding a little more wine if need be, then replace the lid and cook for another 20 minutes. Place the toasted nuts in a blender and blend to form fairly coarse crumbs. Add to the saucepan with the currants and capers and stir everything together well. Taste and adjust the seasoning to your liking. Cook for 2 minutes, then remove the pan from the heat and stir in the lemon juice. Serve straight away with steamed couscous.

Serves 4–6

Pane
CUNZATO *Titone*
TITONE'S BREAD

1 loaf good-quality
sourdough ciabatta

best quality extra-virgin
olive oil

1–2 very ripe tomatoes, sliced

handful fresh basil leaves

salt flakes

This is the snack served by Nicola and Antonella Titone when we went to visit their olive grove. It was so delicious, yet so simple, that I had to include it here.

Slice the ciabatta in half lengthwise. Sprinkle each half with extra-virgin olive oil and top with tomato slices and a few basil leaves, then season with salt flakes.

Serves 4

Involtini
DI *Melanzane*
ROLLED EGGPLANT

3 firm young eggplants

600 ml (20 fl oz)
peanut oil, for frying

2 large fresh mozzarella balls

20 anchovies fillets
in oil, drained

handful fresh basil leaves

salt and freshly
ground black pepper

This dish is great to serve as an appetiser or as part of
an antipasto.

Preheat the oven to 220°C (430°F).

Slice the eggplants lengthwise about 5 mm (¼ in) thick.
You should be able to get around 20 slices in total.

Heat the oil in a large frying pan and when it is hot, fry
the eggplant slices in batches, until golden. Remove them
from the pan and drain on kitchen paper.

Cut each mozzarella ball in half then cut each half into
5 even slices.

Top each slice of eggplant with an anchovy, a slice of mozzarella
and a basil leaf. Season lightly with salt and a few grinds of
pepper. Roll each slice up tightly and secure with a toothpick.

Butter a shallow ovenproof dish. Arrange the involtini in the
dish and bake for 10 minutes, until the mozzarella begins
to melt.

Serves 6

Peperonata

3 large red capsicums
(bell peppers)

3 large yellow capsicums
(bell peppers)

1 large green capsicum
(bell pepper)

SAUCE

50 g (2 oz) pitted black olives

10 anchovy fillets in oil,
drained

140 g (5 oz) capers
in brine, drained

40 g (1½ oz) pine nuts

3 cloves garlic

handful fresh mint leaves

125–200 ml (4–7 fl oz)
virgin olive oil

1 small red chilli

To prepare the capsicums, sit them directly on the flame of your stove burners. Cook for a few minutes, turning them constantly (use tongs to do this). When the skins are black all over, transfer them to a plastic bag, seal the top and leave them to cool down. The steam that is created will loosen the skin and it will peel away easily.

Peel and deseed the capsicums, then cut each one into 4–6 slices. Pat them dry with kitchen paper and arrange them on a serving platter.

To make the sauce, simply put all the ingredients in a blender and whiz until just amalgamated. Be careful not to over-blend it – you should still see the individual ingredients. Spoon some of the sauce over the capsicums and serve the rest on the side in a little bowl. This dish should be eaten at room temperature.

Serves 6

Cuscus DI *Pesce*

FISH COUSCOUS

FISH STOCK

1.5 kg (3 lb 5 oz) assorted fish such as blue eye, ling, sea bass, red mullet or grouper (use the heads and bones for the stock and reserve the fish fillets for the stew)

1 Spanish onion, quartered

4 celery stalks, roughly cut

3 fresh bay leaves

2 teaspoons salt

FISH STEW

assorted fish fillets (see above), cut into 5 cm (2 in) chunks

60 ml (2 fl oz) virgin olive oil

1 large Spanish onion, finely chopped

the heart from ½ bunch celery (light-green leaves included), finely chopped

3 cloves garlic, sliced

3 fresh bay leaves

400 g (14 oz) canned, crushed Italian tomatoes

1 small red chilli, finely sliced

1 blue swimmer crab (to add sweetness to the stew)

1½ litres (3 pints) fish stock (see above)

salt and pepper

¼ teaspoon saffron powder

500 g (1 lb 2 oz) couscous

In Sicily couscous is made by hand, mixing semolina flour with a little water and saffron. It is rolled between the fingers to form small grains, about half the size of peppercorns, which are left to dry on a big wooden board. It is a lengthy process, so for this dish I have broken with tradition and suggested using good-quality purchased couscous. Ask your fishmonger to clean and fillet the fish, and to keep all the heads and bones for you to use to make the stock.

To make the fish stock, put the fish heads and bones in a large pot and cover with cold water. Add the onion, celery, bay leaves and salt and bring to the boil. Simmer gently for 30 minutes, skimming off any scum that rises to the surface. Remove from the heat and strain through a fine sieve.

To make the stew, heat three-quarters of the olive oil in a large saucepan, add the onion, celery and garlic and fry gently for a few minutes until they soften. Add the bay leaves, tomatoes and chilli and simmer gently for about 15 minutes. Add the fish fillets to the pan, together with the crab. Cook for a few minutes then ladle in the fish stock, reserving 600 ml (20 fl oz) for the couscous, and simmer for 10–15 minutes. Taste, then season to your liking with salt and pepper.

Heat the reserved fish stock in a separate saucepan. Stir in the saffron powder then add the couscous. Add the remaining oil, stir well and leave to absorb (as per the packet instructions). Fluff the couscous up with a fork, adding a little more oil if need be. Tip the couscous out onto a warm serving plate and ladle on some of the fish stew. Serve the remaining fish stew on the side.

Serves 6

Cannoli

PASTRY

25 g (1 oz) unsalted butter
at room temperature
(traditionally lard is used
instead of butter)

150 g (5 oz) self-raising flour

1 organic egg, separated

1 tablespoon caster
(superfine) sugar

80 ml (3 fl oz) dry Marsala

pinch of salt

2 tablespoons bitter
cocoa powder

sunflower oil for frying

icing (confectioner's) sugar
for dusting

FILLING

250 g (9 oz) fresh ricotta

125 g (4 oz) icing
(confectioner's) sugar

30 g (1 oz) dark chocolate (70%
cocoa solids), chopped small

finely grated zest of
1 organic lemon

finely grated zest of
1 organic orange

Cannoli are a Sicilian classic and well known all over the world. No Godfather *film would be complete without at least one scene containing this delicious pastry!*

For this recipe you will need to buy special metal cylinders (readily available from specialist cookware shops) to form the pastry tubes.

To make the pastry, put the butter, flour, egg yolk, sugar, Marsala, salt and cocoa powder into a food processor and pulse to form a dough. It will be smooth and firm, similar to pasta dough. Form it into a ball and let it rest, covered with a cloth, for about 1 hour.

While the dough is resting, make the ricotta filling. Whisk the ricotta with the sugar until it is light and fluffy. Mix in the chocolate and citrus zests, then refrigerate until needed.

Roll the pastry out to about 3 mm ($\frac{1}{8}$ in) thick (I find it easiest to feed it through a pasta machine). Cut the pastry into 8 cm ($3\frac{1}{4}$ in) squares and lay them out on a floured work surface. Brush the metal cannoli cylinders lightly with oil. Wrap a piece of pastry on the diagonal around each cylinder. Use the egg white leftover from making the pastry to moisten the edges where they overlap, and press them together gently to seal.

Pour the sunflower oil into a medium-sized saucepan to a depth of around 6 cm. When the oil is hot, fry the cannoli in batches of 3 until golden brown. Drain well on kitchen paper and slide them off the metal cylinders while still warm.

When the cannoli are completely cold, spoon the ricotta filling into a piping bag and fill the cannoli shells generously. Dust with icing sugar and serve. They are best eaten on the day they are made.

Makes around 12 cannoli

Pasta
SICILY'S GIFT TO THE *World*

I AM GOING TO BE A LITTLE CONTROVERSIAL HERE, AND WILL NO DOUBT reveal my own personal bias. But from what I have read and heard, I am convinced that pasta as we know it today originated in Sicily. It is Sicily's gift to the world.

When I say 'pasta', I mean the pasta you find in packets at your local delicatessen or supermarket. This is what Italians call 'pasta asciutta' (dried pasta), to distinguish it from fresh pasta that is made with eggs and must be eaten before it dries. You can find versions of fresh pasta in many different food cultures, usually in the form of doughs that are cooked to make dumplings, flat breads or gnocchi-style dishes. They have existed in the Mediterranean world since time immemorial.

The great virtue of pasta asciutta is that once it has been dried, it can be kept for a long time. Some people, speculating on its origins, say it was created as a food for ships at sea or by nomads, but the evidence seems to say otherwise.

Firstly, to make pasta asciutta you need a special variety of wheat that is quite difficult to mill. This is a particularly hard wheat called 'grano duro' in Italian (we call it durum wheat). Grano duro is high in protein and gluten and has a low moisture content. The protein helps it to dry properly and the gluten gives it the slightly

Opposite: Wheatfields and vines outside Marsala

Above and opposite:
Durum wheat being
milled at Molino IMMA

chewy texture that true pasta asciutta should have. The popular shapes that pasta asciutta took, such as thin noodles (spaghetti), thicker noodles with holes through the middle (macaroni or bucatini) or thin flat sheets (lasagna or canelloni), came about so that the pasta would dry completely. The gnocchi-type balls of pasta frescha would not have dried in the middle so that shape could not be used.

Sicily has been the main source of durum wheat in the Mediterranean world since Roman times. The heat of Sicilian summers and the fertility of the soils gave the island a product no-one else could match.

The second piece of evidence supporting Sicilian pasta is to do with the milling process. Durum wheat is not easy to process and needs hard, heavy millstones. This is difficult on a small scale and ideally is done in a larger, centralised mill with a ready source of power. In an Arab text dating from 1150 there is a reference to just such a mill at Trabia, outside Palermo, which was powered by streams from the mountains behind. The same text mentions 'many shiploads' of dried pasta sent to other places. You can read the full story in John Dickie's fascinating book, *Delizia!: The Epic History of Italians and Their Food.*

There is no evidence of pasta asciutta being produced anywhere else in the Mediterranean, so it seems most likely that it originated in Sicily and gradually spread to the Italian mainland where it evolved and acquired its current position as a signature dish of la cucina Italiana. On the mainland pasta was called many things, but it was often referred to as 'macaroni Siciliani' (Sicilian macaroni), and Sicilians themselves were called, a bit disparagingly, 'macaroni eaters'. Diners in those times clearly thought pasta came from Sicily.

One myth can be laid to rest: pasta did not come from China with Marco Polo. It was established in parts of Italy well before he returned from his travels. Also, Chinese noodles are not made from hard wheat, but from a soft variety; they are quite a different product. Some historians also believe that what Marco Polo was talking about was not wheat-based noodles at all, but sago. Of course for Italians, this is not just a fine point of history, it is a point of honour.

One of the best places to see the famous wheat fields of Sicily is the area inland from Marsala and the south coast of the island. Between the mountainous interior and the coast there are long, spreading river valleys where wheat can be grown on

Above: Sheep with their shepherd, near Marsala
Opposite: Spring haymaking

the flats or on gently sloping hills. In springtime, the crop starts turning gold and wildflowers grow along the walls and roads, their disorder in rich contrast to the ordered uniformity of the wheat.

As you drive through the countryside you will occasionally see flocks of local sheep with a shepherd. Sicilian sheep are raised mainly for their milk as their wool is rough and meat is a luxury that is eaten only at major celebrations like Easter. Curiously, spaghetti with meatballs is often regarded as a typically Sicilian dish but it is not. It actually originated with Sicilian immigrants to New York as a way of showing how rich they were – they could eat meat all the time.

When you see sheep and wheat together, you are seeing two of the raw materials for a typical pasta dish: wheat for the pasta itself and sheep for pecorino, the salty sheep's milk cheese that you grate over it. It must be said that these days Parmesan cheese is also widely used in Sicilian cooking, as well as pecorino. But Parmesan is a product from the valley of the River Po in the north of Italy, not local to Sicily at all. It is an exceptional cheese, though, and it must have been its taste that overcame the skepticism of locals about a 'mainland' product.

Every Sicilian grows (or seems to know someone who grows) tomatoes, the third element in the mix. Typically tomatoes used to make a pasta sauce are cooked down to a concentrated spiced paste. In Sicilian markets you will see slabs of a thick, almost dry tomato paste called strattu, which is used for the classic pasta al pomodoro sauce.

One rather surprising and very distinctive thing about pasta dishes in Sicily is that they are often served with breadcrumbs. In fact quite a number of other dishes also use breadcrumbs, either as a crumb coating or in a stuffing. The reason is simple but sad. For a long time the price of pasta was a lot higher than the price of bread – it was considered something of a luxury dish. If you were a poor person (and poverty was widespread on the island until the 1960s) you would use your leftover bread to make the pasta go further. When bread was used in stuffings, it was to make the dish more filling. Hunger was a key element in the Sicilian diet. But in more prosperous times, Sicilians have acquired the taste for breadcrumbs and bread stuffings and use them not because they are hungry but because they like

Above: Wheat on a terraced hillside with poppies
Opposite: An abundance of tomatoes

Pasta  alle Sarde

PASTA WITH FRESH SARDINES

600 g (1 lb 5 oz) fresh sardines

2 tablespoons salt

2 big bunches wild fennel

150 ml (5 fl oz)
virgin olive oil

1 large Spanish onion,
finely chopped

1 teaspoon ground cumin

1 teaspoon ground cinnamon

1 teaspoon turmeric

1 teaspoon ground ginger

5 anchovy fillets in oil, drained

50 g (2 oz) currants

50 g (2 oz) pine nuts, toasted

100 g (3½ oz) fresh
breadcrumbs

1 handful Italian
flat-leaf parsley, chopped

1 handful mint, chopped

1 handful marjoram, chopped

½ teaspoon saffron powder

salt and pepper

500 g (1 lb 2 oz) strozzapreti
or bucatini

*For many Sicilians, this is the island's 'signature' pasta dish,
full of typical Moorish flavours.*

Scrape away the scales from the sardines. Pull the heads away
from the bodies – the backbones will naturally come away too.
Your fishmonger will do this for you if you prefer. Dry the
sardines well on kitchen paper.

Add the salt to a large saucepan of water and bring to the boil.
Drop in the fennel and simmer for 5 minutes. Lift it out of the
water and chop finely. Reserve the water for cooking the pasta.

To make the sauce, heat 3 tablespoons of the olive oil in a large
frying pan. Add the onion and cook until soft and translucent. Stir
in the spices and cook for a few more minutes. Add the anchovies,
currants, pine nuts and half the sardines. Cook for around
5 minutes, stirring and breaking up the sardines with a fork.

Add the breadcrumbs, chopped fennel, herbs and saffron to the
pan with another 2 tablespoons of olive oil. Season to taste and
cook for a further 1–2 minutes.

Boil the pasta in the reserved fennel water until it is cooked
al dente.

Meanwhile, heat 2 tablespoons of the olive oil in a separate frying
pan and quickly fry the remaining sardines until golden.

Drain the pasta and tip half into a warm serving bowl. Stir in the
rest of the olive oil and half of the sauce. Top with the remaining
sauce and the fried sardines and toss together at the table.

Serves 4–6

Pasta
ALLA *Bottarga*
PASTA WITH
SUN-DRIED MULLET ROE

500 g (1 lb 2 oz) spaghetti

190 ml (5–6½ fl oz) virgin olive oil

10 anchovy fillets in oil, drained

50 g (2 oz) fresh breadcrumbs

2 tablespoons baby capers in brine, drained

½ bunch Italian flat-leaf parsley, chopped

½ bunch fresh mint, chopped

20 cherry tomatoes, halved

100 g (3½ oz) bottarga (sun-dried mullet roe), membrane removed, shaved or very finely grated

salt and pepper

I think it is important in certain dishes to balance the flavours. More is not necessarily always better, as is demonstrated in this recipe.

Boil the pasta in plenty of salted water.

While the pasta is cooking, heat 2 tablespoons of the olive oil in a small frying pan. Add the anchovies and stir them around in the oil until they melt. Add the breadcrumbs, capers, parsley and mint and toss over the heat for about 2 minutes, taking care not to burn the breadcrumbs. Remove the pan from the heat.

As soon as the pasta is cooked al dente, drain it, reserving about ½ cup of the cooking water. Tip the pasta into a warm serving dish and stir in the reserved water. Stir in the remaining olive oil then add the breadcrumb mixture, tomatoes and bottarga. Toss everything together gently, then taste and adjust the seasoning to your liking. Serve immediately.

Serves 4–6

Pasta *Primavera*

PASTA WITH SPRING VEGETABLES

50 g (2 oz) unsalted butter

3 baby leeks, trimmed
and sliced

2 cloves garlic, crushed

1 small fennel bulb,
very thinly sliced

1½ tablespoons salt

150 g (5 oz) podded baby broad
beans, blanched and peeled

150 g (5 oz) baby French beans,
cut into 3 cm (1¼ in) lengths

150 g (5 oz) podded fresh peas

1 bunch thin asparagus, cut
into 3 cm (1¼ in) lengths

400 ml (14 fl oz) pure cream

500 g (1 lb 2 oz) ditali pasta
(small 1 cm tubes)

salt and freshly ground
black pepper

100 g (3½ oz) freshly grated
Parmiggiano

Melt the butter in a large frying pan. Add the leeks and cook gently for 5 minutes, then add the garlic and fennel and cook until soft.

Add the salt to a large saucepan of water and bring to the boil. When the water boils, drop in the broad beans, French beans, peas and asparagus. As soon as the water comes back to the boil, lift the vegetables out with a slotted spoon (reserve the water for cooking the pasta) and add them to the frying pan with the leek and fennel mixture. Pour in the cream and bring to the boil.

Let it bubble for 2 minutes – the vegetables should still have a crunch – then remove the pan from the heat.

Boil the pasta in the vegetable water until al dente.

Drain the pasta well and add to the cream and vegetable mix. Toss everything together. Season with salt and pepper, add the Parmiggiano and serve straight away.

Serves 4–6

Pasta
CON PESTO ALLA *Trapanese*
PASTA WITH PESTO, TRAPANI-STYLE

PESTO

1 bunch fresh basil, leaves only

6 very ripe tomatoes, skin and seeds removed, roughly chopped

50 g (2 oz) fresh almonds

1–2 cloves garlic, crushed

50 g (2 oz) fresh breadcrumbs

125 ml (4 fl oz) virgin olive oil

salt and pepper

500 g (1 lb 2 oz) spaghettini or spaghetti

100 g (3½ oz) dried salted ricotta, or Parmiggiano freshly grated

This pesto is delicious made with the fresh, young almonds that are available in late spring. At other times of the year you can use ordinary almonds.

To make the pesto, put all the ingredients into a mortar or food processor and blitz to a coarse paste. Taste and adjust the seasoning to your liking.

Boil the pasta in plenty of salted water. As soon as the pasta is cooked al dente, drain it and tip it into a warm serving dish. Pour on the pesto and toss well. Take to the table straight away and serve with the ricotta or Parmiggiano on the side.

Serves 4–6

Pesto
AL *Pistacchio*
PISTACHIO PESTO

250 g (9 oz) unsalted pistachio nuts, lightly toasted

50 g (2 oz) capers in brine, drained

50 g (2 oz) anchovy fillets in oil, drained

2 cloves garlic

1 small red chilli

125 ml (4 fl oz) virgin olive oil

This pesto is great to serve with pasta or grilled vegetables.

Put all the ingredients into your food processor and blend to a smooth paste. Serve straight away or keep in the refrigerator for up to a week.

Makes around 400 g (14 oz) pesto

Pesto
AI CAPPERI E *Mandorle*
CAPER AND ALMOND PESTO

250 g (9 oz) almonds,
lightly toasted

250 g (9 oz) capers
in brine, drained

1–2 small red chillies
(depending on how
hot you like it)

2 cloves garlic

250 ml (8½ fl oz)
virgin olive oil

salt and pepper

Put all the ingredients into your food processor and blend
to a chunky paste. Do not over-process this pesto as I think
it is best if you can still see small chunks of the almonds
and capers.

Makes around 750 g (1 lb 10 oz) pesto

Pasta
AL BORGO SAN *Nicolao*
PASTA WITH CREAM AND SPECK

500 g (1 lb 2 oz) macaroni

50 g (2 oz) unsalted butter

8 thin slices of speck, diced

1 small red chilli, finely
chopped (optional)

½ teaspoon saffron powder

1 bunch Italian flat-leaf
parsley, chopped

300 ml (10½ fl oz) pure cream

salt and pepper

150 g (5 oz) pecorino, grated

*I like to use the De Cecco brand of pasta because it comes from
Sicily and I find it stays al dente.*

Boil the pasta in plenty of salted water.

While the pasta is cooking, melt the butter in a frying pan and fry
the speck for a few minutes. If you are using chilli, add it now, then
add the saffron, parsley and cream and let it just come to the boil.

As soon as the pasta is cooked al dente, drain it and tip it into a
warm serving dish.

Pour the hot sauce over the pasta and toss well. Taste and
adjust the seasoning to your liking, then add the pecorino
and serve immediately.

Serves 4–6

Modica and Noto

THE LAND OF THE *Baroque*

IN 1693 A MASSIVE EARTHQUAKE DEVASTATED A NUMBER OF CITIES IN southeastern Sicily. What was a disaster then has now become a source of delight, as the cities were rebuilt in the Spanish baroque style and are today extraordinary examples of that period.

It is unusual to find a whole city built in one style at one time, and to find them built in Spanish baroque style, with all its flourishes and extravagances, is something of a wonder. The cities of Palazzola, Ragusa and Ispica all contain wonderful baroque buildings, but it is the cities of Modica and Noto that are my favourites.

The main street in Modica runs along the bottom of a steep-walled valley. Both sides of the valley are almost completely built up, with the grandest houses and churches situated near the main street, the lesser ones rising up the hills. Along the valley, small squares are filled with fountains and statues and broad flights of steps lead up to the next level. With the quality of its buildings, the unity of its architecture and the very human scale, the old centre of Modica is delightful.

Perhaps in keeping with the frills of its architecture, Modica is known for its confectionery, and in particular for a local chocolate made from carob beans. Carob

Opposite: Rooftops, Modica

*Above: Carob trees,
pods and 'chocolate'
Opposite: Modica*

trees, like olives, are enormously tough and can grow to a great age. They grow on stony terrain in the area between Modica and the coast to the south, some clearly hundreds of years old. Over centuries of labour, local stone has been collected to build a network of walls that must stretch for over a hundred kilometres. The country here is divided into small fields bounded by these walls. The fields are planted with carob trees with grazing land beneath them. With the old stone walls and old carob trees, it is a remarkable landscape.

Carob chocolate is made from the pods of the tree and is dark, hard and brittle. It is sweetened with sugar and scented with cinnamon and orange. Despite its name, if you think of carob as chocolate, you will be disappointed. It is nothing like the smooth, rich, melt-in-the-mouth chocolate from the more familiar cocoa bean. Think of it instead as a type of spiced confectionery bar that is at its best when grated over pastry desserts and ice creams.

Modica has a reputation for the quality of its pasticcerie, where you can buy pastries, confectionery and ice cream. My favourite is the Chantilly pasticceria—gelateria on Corso Umberto, the main street. It is here that Angelo Cataldi and his

STRADA
CAMPAILLA

Chantilly

*Above: Angelo Cataldi
and Maria Concetta at
Pasticceria Chantilly,
Modica*

wife, Maria Concetta, work their magic. All the pastries are fine and delicate. There is an enormous variety of small marzipan fruits and a familiar range of ice creams, some in tiny cones, with the pastel colours of the ice creams dusted with ground pistachio. The shop is a delight and totally in keeping with the baroque flourishes of Modica itself.

Pasticcerie in Sicily have a rather unusual history. Although their beginnings lie back in the time of the Moors with the introduction of sugarcane to the island, today's more refined sweets were developed several centuries later, in the many convents around the island.

It is thought likely that the convents started creating elaborate marzipan fruits and delicate pastries as a way to celebrate saints' days. One local legend describes how a particular convent created marzipan oranges to hang on an out-of-season orange tree to decorate it for the bishop's visit. Whatever the origins, sweet making soon grew into a source of regular income.

In those days, many of the convents were closed orders, and nuns were not permitted contact with outsiders. So they devised a technique to sell their produce

PASTICCERIA
Grammatico
Maria

without breaking the rules of the order. Their solution was a revolving wheel set in the convent wall – similar to what you sometimes see at a bank counter. The customers were unable to see into the room beyond, so they placed their written request and some money on the wheel and turned it. A short time later the wheel would turn back and their sweets would appear. There was just such a turning wheel in the wall of a convent in central Palermo until only a few years ago.

Quite by chance, I met a woman called Maria Grammatico, who had grown up in a convent where she learned the craft of confectionery and pastry making. Maria had been placed with the nuns as a child, as her mother could not afford to look after her. She lived a very austere life in the convent, and her skill in producing marzipan confectionery and delicate pastries was her one real pleasure. Today Maria is well known for the pasticceria she runs in the town of Erice near Trapani. Erice is an old fortified town spectacularly situated on top of a steep mountain with views of the coast. Maria Grammatico's pasticceria is almost at the top of the mountain and it is visited by most of the people who go to Erice – both to sample its delicacies and to meet a woman of great vitality and charm.

Above: Confectionery
from Pasticceria Maria
Grammatico, Erice
Following pages: The
mountaintop of Erice

On our travels we discovered another wonderful bakery in the small town of Frigintini, outside Modica, where we stopped for a coffee. On finding ourselves outside a flour mill (the Mulino I.M.M.A.), I naturally asked if I might look around. While we were admiring the beautiful grano duro flour, I noticed some sacks of the flour being carried across the road to a small bakery. We followed the trail and entered the realm of Giorgia Colomba, the San Antonio Panificio–Biscottificio (bread and biscuit bakery). At the back of the shop her two assistants, Angela and Graziana, were rolling out pastries and a large oven stood in the next room. As we quickly found out, the house specialty is impanatigghi, a small pastry with a delicious rich filling made from sugar, almonds, chocolate and spices and a small quantity of finely minced lean beef. Rather than giving a meaty taste to the pastries, the beef adds a real richness to the filling – in the same way that suet is used in traditional English Christmas mince pies and puddings.

Not far from Frigintini is the perfect baroque town of Noto. After the earthquake the city was rebuilt in a warm, light-golden stone, and the decoration on the facades of the palaces and churches is the most elaborate you will see anywhere.

Above: Giorgia Colomba (centre) and her assistants making impanatigghi

*Above and opposite:
Baroque splendours
at Noto*

Every balcony seems to be held up by a cast of mythical characters, each one more exotic than the next. If you are in the area then Noto is certainly a 'must' to visit. But on the whole, I find Modica a friendlier and more sympathetic city. Perhaps it's because Modica is less of a museum town than Nota – and the people there are passionate about their city and its food.

One particular incident brought this home to me. I was in a menswear store with my husband who was buying a belt. There were two or three other customers in the store and a couple of attendants. As we were paying I casually asked the store manager where he would recommend we ate that evening. In an instant the atmosphere in the shop changed. Suddenly everyone crowded around the counter offering suggestions, criticising other recommendations and recounting their own experiences. This went on for a good fifteen minutes or so, and at the end of it all we had been given several good ideas, but there was no general consensus. As we were leaving the store we were approached by a distinguished-looking elderly gentleman (I later found out he was Franco Antonio Belgiorno, the author of well-known books on Modica) who advised me, 'The best food in Sicily is eaten at home.'

In keeping with the spirit of Modica and Noto, the recipes I have selected for this chapter are all biscuits or pastries. Firstly there is Maria Grammatico's Ricetta Base, which is the pastry recipe for all her almond pastries, and incredibly useful. She learned this recipe while at the convent of San Carlo.

Sigarette alla Ricotta are similar to the mini cannoli that are the house specialty of pasticceria Amato, behind the Teatro Massimo in Palermo. They are light and delicate and you can flavour the ricotta filling with your choice of candied fruit or chocolate.

I had to include a recipe for Giorgia Colomba's Impanatigghi. Please don't be put off by the inclusion of meat – if you try them I think you will really like them. I have also chosen a recipe for Nnacatuli Liparesi, which are delicious small pastries with a rather exotic filling.

My friend Ada, whose family comes from Italy, makes wonderful almond macaroons so I had to include her recipe. And finally, there is a recipe for little biscuits that I call Cucuricci. It comes from my aunt who lived in Palermo and they are a family favourite.

Nnacatuli *Liparesi*

LITTLE PARCELS FROM LIPARI

PASTRY

500 g (1 lb 2 oz)
self-raising flour

2 organic eggs plus
1 organic egg yolk

60 g (2 oz) caster
(superfine) sugar

150 g (5 oz) unsalted butter
at room temperature

1 teaspoon pure vanilla extract

½ teaspoon salt

STUFFING

200 g (7 oz) ground almonds

200 g (7 oz) caster
(superfine) sugar

2 teaspoons ground cinnamon

few drops of rose water

grated zest of 1 organic lemon

1 organic egg white

Preheat the oven to 200°C (400°F).

To make the pastry, place the ingredients in a food processor and pulse until it all comes together. Roll into a ball, wrap in cling-film and refrigerate for 30 minutes.

To make the stuffing, mix all the ingredients together to form a sticky paste.

Roll the pastry to about 3 mm (¹/8 in) thick on a lightly floured work surface. With a pastry cutter, cut out circles of around 8 cm (3¼ in). Place a teaspoon of stuffing on one side of each pastry circle. Fold the pastry over to create a half moon and use the back of a fork to press around the rim to seal the edges.

Line an oven tray with greaseproof paper. Prick little holes on the top of the biscuits and lift them onto the oven tray. Bake for 6–8 minutes until golden brown. Remove from the oven and transfer to a rack to cool. They will keep in an airtight jar for 4–5 days.

Makes around 25 parcels

Ricetta *Base*

ALMOND PASTRY BASE

450 g (1 lb) almonds, blanched and peeled

450 g (1 lb) caster (superfine) sugar

3 organic egg whites

1 tablespoon honey

1 tablespoon grated organic lemon zest

2 teaspoons almond extract (optional)

icing (confectioner's sugar) for dusting (optional)

This is Maria Grammatico's pastry recipe for her little almond pastries, learned at the convent where she grew up as a girl. She uses it to make sospiri, cuscinetti and desideri. I have used this recipe here to make simple almond biscuits.

Place the almonds in a food processor with half the sugar and process to a fine powder. Tip into a large mixing bowl and add the remaining ingredients. Use your hands to mix everything together well then work it to a nice smooth paste.

Shape into a ball and wrap in cling-film.

Chill the dough for at least 30 minutes. When you are ready to bake the biscuits, preheat the oven to 180°C and line an oven tray with greaseproof paper. Roll the pastry into little balls of about 2 cm (¾ in) diameter and place them on the tray. Bake for about 12 minutes until they are golden.

While they are still warm, you can dust them with icing sugar.

Note

The pastry will keep in the refrigerator for up to 3 days.

Makes around 900 g (2 lb) pastry

Sigarette
ALLA *Ricotta*
RICOTTA-FILLED CIGARETTES

60 g (2 oz) unsalted butter at room temperature

75 g (2½ oz) caster (superfine) sugar

45 g (1½ oz) unbleached plain flour

½ teaspoon pure vanilla extract

2 organic egg whites, beaten to stiff peaks

icing (confectioner's) sugar for dusting

RICOTTA FILLING

250 g (9 oz) very fresh full-cream ricotta

2 tablespoons caster (superfine) sugar

These are small, light, cigarette-shaped pastries. They are delicious served with an espresso at the end of a meal, or just as a little treat during the day.

Preheat the oven to 200°C (400°F).

Beat the butter and sugar until light and fluffy. Stir in the flour and vanilla extract, then gently fold in the egg whites.

Line two oven trays with greaseproof paper. Place small, well-spaced spoonfuls of the pastry mixture onto the trays and spread them out to form 6 cm (2½ in) circles. Bake for 5 minutes until the biscuits are golden. Remove from the oven and while still warm, carefully roll the biscuits around the handle of a wooden spoon to form 'cigarettes'. Slide them off and leave them to cool completely.

To make the filling, beat the ricotta with the sugar to make a smooth, lump-free cream.

When the cigarettes are completely cold, spoon the ricotta filling into a piping bag and fill them generously. Dust with icing sugar and serve straight away.

Variation

If you like, add 2 tablespoons of grated lemon or orange zest or 2 tablespoons of grated chocolate to the ricotta filling.

Makes 18–20 little cigarettes

Impanatigghi

PASTRY

300 g (10½ oz)
unbleached plain flour

150 g (5 oz) unsalted butter at
room temperature

80 g (3 oz) caster
(superfine) sugar

1 organic egg,
plus 1 organic egg yolk

½ teaspoon salt

grated zest of 1 organic lemon

FILLING

250 g (9 oz) ground almonds

150 g (5 oz) caster
(superfine) sugar

grated zest of 1 organic lemon

2 teaspoons ground cinnamon

50 g (2 oz) finely
minced lean beef

100 g (3½ oz) dark
chocolate, melted

few drops of Marsala
(if necessary)

Don't be put off by the fact that these biscuits contain a little minced beef in the filling. It is an old and very traditional Modica recipe and the biscuits were made to be nutritious. It is similar to using suet in your Christmas mince pies: you don't actually taste the meat itself, but somehow the overall flavour is intensified.

Preheat the oven to 180°C (350°F).

To make the pastry, place the ingredients in a food processor and pulse until it all comes together. Roll into a ball, wrap in clingfilm and refrigerate for 30 minutes.

To make the filling, mix all the ingredients together well to form a thickish paste. If it seems too dry, add a few drops of Marsala.

Roll the pastry out as thinly as you can on a lightly floured work surface. With a pastry cutter, cut out circles of around 6 cm (2½ in). With a sharp knife make a small 1 cm (½ in) incision along the bottom third of each circle.

Spoon the filling into a piping bag and pipe around 2½ cm (1 in) of filling widthways across the centre of each pastry circle, parallel with the incision. Brush the rim with a little water, then fold the pastry over to create a half moon. Make sure the little cut is uppermost. Press around the rim to seal and trim away any excess pastry. Crimp the edge with the back of a fork.

Line an oven tray with greaseproof paper. Lift the filled biscuits onto the tray and bake for 15–20 minutes until golden brown. Remove from the oven and transfer to a rack to cool. They will keep in an airtight jar for about a week.

Makes around 20 biscuits

Macaroncini
DI *Ada*
ADA'S MACAROONS

2 organic egg whites

300 g (10½ oz)
ground almonds

250 g (9 oz) icing
(confectioner's) sugar

pinch of salt

finely grated zest of
1 organic lemon

*This recipe was given to me by my friend Ada, the queen
of macaroons!*

Beat the egg whites until they form stiff peaks. Fold in the
almonds, sugar, salt and lemon zest.

Line 2 baking trays with greaseproof paper. With wet hands,
take small portions of the mixture and roll into 2½ cm (1 in)
balls between your palms. Pinch the tops of the balls and arrange
them on the baking trays. Refrigerate for 30 minutes before
baking, which will make them spread less.

Preheat the oven to 180°C (350°F).

Bake the macaroons for 10 minutes, or until they are just starting
to colour. Remove from the oven and leave the macaroons to
cool for a few minutes on the tray before transferring to a rack.
When the macaroons are completely cold, transfer them to an
airtight container. They will keep for up to a week.

Variation

*Push a few almond slivers into the top of each macaroon
before baking.*

Makes around 30 biscuits

Cucuricci

250 g (9 oz) unsalted butter
at room temperature

280 g (10 oz) unbleached
plain flour

150 g (5 oz) caster
(superfine) sugar

250 g (9 oz) almonds, toasted
and coarsely ground

grated zest of 1 organic lemon

1 teaspoon pure lemon oil

1 teaspoon baking powder

pinch of salt

icing (confectioner's) sugar
for dusting (optional)

*These biscuits are a great family favourite. The recipe comes
from my aunt, who lived in Palermo.*

Preheat the oven to 180°C (350°F).

Mix all the ingredients, except for the icing sugar, in an electric
mixer. Stop as soon as they are amalgamated; it is important not
to overwork the dough.

Line a baking tray with greaseproof paper. Form the biscuits
into little almond shapes, around 3½ x 1½ cm (1½ x ¾ in)
and arrange on the baking tray. Bake for 8 minutes, or until the
biscuits begin to turn a pale gold. Remove from the oven
and lift them onto a rack to cool.

Dust with icing sugar if you like and store in an airtight jar.

Makes around 40 biscuits

The Cheeses OF *Sicily*

ONE AFTERNOON DURING MY VISIT TO MODICA, AS I WAS STROLLING DOWN the Corso Umberto I, I spotted a tiny cheese shop. It was so small that if you weren't looking carefully you would miss it. Inside the spotless, white-tiled shop was a refrigerated cabinet stocked with a range of local cheeses. As it turned out, this was the retail outlet of a local farm, and so, my curiosity aroused, I went to visit the farm the very next day.

We rose early – because like milking, cheese making is done early in the day – and drove out of town onto a plateau of rolling hills. Farmhouses dotted the landscape and stone terraces and walls testified to the effort that had been put into the land over a long time. The fields themselves were covered in poppies. Others had been cut for hay and animals grazed on the crop stubble. It was a timeless scene of farms in late spring.

But once you have travelled through the Sicilian countryside for a while, you realise how unusual this picture really is. Because so much of the rural land has traditionally been held as vast estates by absentee owners, you don't actually see large farmhouses very often. There are villages (for the estate workers), the occasional

Opposite: Countryside near Modica

Above: Old farmhouses
Opposite: Cheese
making at the
Lucifora family farm

palazzo (for the landowner) but very few of the manor houses or groups of farm buildings that you associate with a prosperous family farm.

The countryside outside Modica is somewhat different, and is clearly populated by family farms. As we drove towards our destination we passed substantial two-storey houses, surrounded by high walls and a cluster of work buildings. Standing either side of the entrance would often be two date palms with their tall, straight trunks finishing in a burst of spreading fronds, which look for all the world like botanical fireworks. I don't know why, historically, this area has developed differently from other parts of the country, but it does make you aware of the gap that exists in the social fabric elsewhere.

About fifteen kilometres out of Modica we arrived at the farm of the Lucifora family. Outside the dairy Salvatore Lucifora was looking after seventy or so milking cows. The farmyard was surrounded by terraces planted with grains, olive, almond and carob trees. Inside the dairy we found his wife Ornella and her cheese maker, Raimondo Blandino. Cheese making was in full swing, and had been since three o'clock that morning.

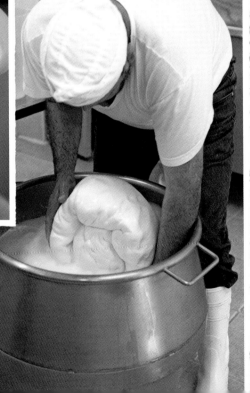

Cheese in Sicily is made from cow's, sheep's and goat's milk. It is an ancient art – there are records of hard cheese being made in Roman times. Sicilian cheeses range from seasoned hard cheeses to delicate fresh ones, and everything in between. The most famous cheese made in Sicily, the most 'tipico', is ricotta. It is emblematic of the island and is the key ingredient in local specialties such as cassata and cannoli. In my view, it is hard to find a fresher or lighter cheese anywhere in the world.

For such an important cheese, it is fascinating to discover that ricotta is actually a by-product: it is made from the whey that is leftover from making other cheeses. Ricotta needs to be eaten fresh, so in the days before refrigeration it was only produced seasonally, not in the hot summer months. As a result, cheese makers developed techniques to preserve it, such as smoking, salting or baking. All these varieties are interesting cheeses, but without a doubt, the full ricotta experience can only be had from the super-fresh product.

It is traditional Sicilian hospitality to offer a guest a bowl of warm, fresh ricotta and this is what Ornella did. She spooned fresh ricotta into terracotta bowls and we ate it with fresh bread that had been quickly dipped into the water that drained

from the cheese. This is the way ricotta has been eaten for centuries, and if you try it like this, you can see why it is so prized. Ricotta is delicious cooked or flavoured and sugared in cakes and pastries, but for me, the pure experience of eating fresh ricotta, untreated in any way, is unique.

Next door Raimondo was hard at work making Caciocavallo cheese. His arms were plunged up to the elbows in a vat of water, heated to 60–70°C, and he was kneading the cheese into a large ball. The kneading process lasted for about forty minutes until there were no air pockets left in the large round cheese. It was then ready to be soaked in brine for two or three days before being hung by its distinctive top-knot to mature. The finished cheeses have a medium–hard consistency and weigh between 16–17 kilograms.

A few days later I visited another cheese factory at Randazzo near Mount Etna. Here I watched another cheese maker, Santo La Mancusa, making his version of Caciocavallo. Santo was taught by his father, who had only just retired. While he himself is young (in his thirties), he told me that he worries that cheese-making skills are not being passed on anymore as young people find it too much work.

Above: Modica streets

As well as Caciocavallo, Santo makes Tuma cheese (which is another medium–hard cheese that can be round or squared) and beautiful fresh ricotta.

The area around Modica and the nearby city of Ragusa is well known for the quality of its cheeses and the skill of its cheese makers. You get a feel for this if you visit Casa del Formaggio (the House of Cheese), an exceptional cheese shop in Modica, owned by Giorgio Cannata. As I entered the shop I was encouraged by a sign in the window, indicating that he was a Slow Food-approved retailer. The Slow Food movement started in Piemonte and has since spread all over Italy and around the world. It is dedicated to preserving the crafts of traditional food production and aims to encourage everything that mass-produced, standardised, homogenised food production is not. The Slow Food movement treats small-scale traditional cheese-makers as an endangered species – and they are right to do so. The organisation sends people out to record the special cheeses, to note how they are made, who are making them and which specialised retailers are selling them.

As soon as I walked into Giorgio's shop I could tell he was passionate about his products. Most of the cheeses he stocks are Sicilian, the majority from the south

of the island nearby. There is a huge range of Caciocavallo and Tuma cheeses, and many Pecorini and other hard, long-matured cheeses. There are ricottas that have been salted, smoked or baked and there are highly seasonal spring cheeses that can only be made when grasses are long and lush. At his suggestion we tried a selection of cheeses, but our favourite arrived in the middle of the tasting. It was a Formaggio Nero, a large cheese with a black rind that comes from the area inland from Agrigento and is only made in small amounts. It was semi-seasoned, lightly salted and totally delicious.

Believe it or not fresh ricotta is pretty simple to make. So if you can't find it in a shop or market near you, or even if you can, you might like to try making it yourself. My friend Maria has a simple way to do it and I have included her recipe. She uses sheep's milk, but it is also excellent when made with full-cream, pasteurised cow's milk.

Once you have made fresh ricotta and tasted it with crusty bread, what are you going to cook with it? I have included some ricotta recipes earlier in the book, but there are a few more in this chapter for you to experiment with.

First, there is a wonderful savoury ricotta pie called Torta Rustica alla Ricotta. The ricotta is mixed with salty pecorino cheese, eggs and ham. Although it is a little bit like a quiche, it is much lighter – that's the great virtue of ricotta. It makes a delicious lunch with salad.

Ricotta is often used to add richness to other sauces and dishes, but also to lighten them. I particularly love meatballs made with ricotta because it gives them quite another consistency. Polpettine con Ricotta (meatballs with ricotta) are light and tasty.

Some of the other Sicilian cheeses are also excellent to cook with so I have included two recipes, one using Caciocavallo, the other pecorino. Caciu all'Argintera (pan-fried cheese) uses Caciocavallo to make a great antipasto dish. Carciofi Ripieni (stuffed artichokes) combines pecorino with anchovies and capers – all sharp, salty flavours – and breadcrumbs to make a stuffing for tender young artichokes.

Cheese is not the only product of the Modica region. Chocolate is used often (a legacy of Spanish rule, introduced by them from South America), as are almonds. Superb almonds are grown near Avola on the nearby coast; in fact Avola almonds are said to be the best in Sicily. I have included a recipe that combines both these ingredients in a delectable Crostata di Amaretti e Cioccolato (a tart made with an amaretti and chocolate filling).

*Above: Countryside
outside Modica
Opposite: Goats and
sheep cared for by
a stylish shepherd*

Ricotta

DI *Maria*

MARIA'S RICOTTA

1 litre (2 pints) full-cream milk

80 ml (2½ fl oz) white flavourless vinegar

180 ml (6 fl oz) water

salt to taste (optional)

My friend Maria taught me to make this ricotta. She usually uses sheep's milk, but the recipe here uses pasteurised cow's milk and it works very well. In Sicily they like their ricotta a little salty.

Heat the milk in a large saucepan, stirring constantly. As soon as it boils, remove the pan from the heat.

Mix the vinegar and water together in a small jug. Pour it into the milk in a slow, steady stream, beginning in the centre then working out in a bigger and bigger circle until you reach the edge of the pan. You will see the milk start to separate.

Sit the saucepan in a sink of very cold water. After a few minutes use a slotted spoon to lift the ricotta out and transfer to a colander lined with a damp cheesecloth. Sit the colander on a plate and leave to drain. If you are not using it straight away, transfer to the refrigerator.

The watery liquid that remains behind in the pan is called the whey. If it still looks a little cloudy and milky, return it to the boil. You will see it coagulate to form a little more ricotta. Put the pan back into the sink of cold water and lift the ricotta out with a slotted spoon and transfer to the colander.

The whey may be combined with more milk to make further batches of ricotta. I actually find the second, third and fourth batches are better, as they loose some of the acidity of the vinegar. If you don't plan to make more ricotta straight away, you can pour the whey into a glass jar and keep it in the refrigerator for up to 4 days.

Makes around 100g (3½ oz)

Torta
RUSTICA ALLA *Ricotta*
RICOTTA PIE

PASTRY

500 g (1 lb 2 oz)
unbleached plain flour

150 g (5 oz) unsalted butter
at room temperature

1 organic egg

125 ml (4 fl oz)
medium–dry Marsala

50 g (2 oz) freshly
grated pecorino

1 teaspoon salt

freshly ground black pepper

FILLING

500 g (1 lb 2 oz)
fresh full-cream ricotta

150 g (5 oz) prosciutto,
cut into strips

100 g (3½ oz) freshly
grated Parmiggiano

100 g (3½ oz) pecorino
piccante, grated

2 organic eggs

freshly ground black pepper

This dish can be served as a main dish for lunch, or as part of an antipasto selection.

To make the pastry, put all the ingredients into a food processor and pulse until the dough is just amalgamated. Roll it into a ball and place it in the refrigerator to rest for an hour.

Preheat the oven to 200°C (400°F) and butter a 23 cm (9 in) ovenproof dish.

Break off just over half of the pastry and roll it out on a lightly floured work surface to about 5 mm (¼ in) thick then lift it into the prepared dish so the pastry comes up the sides.

Mix all the filling ingredients together and season with pepper. The cheeses and prosciutto are fairly salty, so don't add any salt. Pour the filling into the pastry and smooth the surface.

Roll out the remaining pastry and use it to cover the pie. Press around the rim to seal the edges and prick the pie lid all over with a fork. Transfer to the oven and bake for 30 minutes or until golden brown. Remove the pie from the oven and leave it to cool down completely before serving. If it is still warm, the ricotta will be too runny to cut into beautiful slices.

Serves 4

Polpettine
CON *Ricotta*
MEATBALLS WITH RICOTTA

800 g (1 lb 12 oz) minced lamb

300 g (10½ oz) fresh ricotta

50 g (2 oz) freshly
grated Parmiggiano

100 g (3½ oz) unsalted butter

75 ml (2½ fl oz)
virgin olive oil

1 large Spanish onion,
finely chopped

3 cloves garlic, crushed

2 teaspoons ground cumin

1 teaspoon ground coriander

1 teaspoon ground cinnamon

2 fresh rosemary sprigs,
stalks discarded and
leaves chopped

½ bunch Italian flat-leaf
parsley, finely chopped

100 g (3½ oz) pine nuts

60 g (2 oz) fresh breadcrumbs

2 organic eggs

salt and pepper

Place the minced lamb and cheeses into a large mixing bowl.
Heat around 20 g (¾ oz) of the butter and 2 tablespoons of the
oil in a frying pan. Add the onion and cook over a low heat until
it softens. Add the garlic, spices, herbs and pine nuts and cook
for another 5 minutes, stirring frequently. Remove the pan from
the heat and leave to cool.

Add the breadcrumbs and eggs to the lamb and cheese then tip
in the spicy onion mixture and season with salt and pepper. Use
your hands to mix everything together well. At this stage you can
cover the mince mixture and leave it in the refrigerator for a few
hours, or even overnight, until needed.

Roll spoonfuls of the mince into small balls between the palms
of your hands.

Fry the meatballs in batches using the remaining butter and oil,
turning onto all sides until they are golden brown. Transfer to a
serving dish and keep warm in the oven.

The meatballs are delicious served hot, warm or cold. If you
like, serve them with the Tomato Sauce from Natalia's Timballo
(page 27).

Serves 6

Caciu

ALL'Argintera

PAN-FRIED CHEESE

60 ml (2 fl oz) extra-virgin
olive oil

3 cloves garlic,
roughly chopped

4 slices of Caciocavallo,
around 1½ cm (¾ in) thick

2 tablespoons white
balsamic vinegar

1 tablespoon chopped
oregano leaves

freshly ground black pepper

Caciocavallo is a traditional medium–hard Sicilian cheese.
This is a very simple but delicious recipe for a light lunch.
Heat the oil in a large frying pan over a gentle heat. Fry the
garlic until it begins to turn pale gold then discard it.
Increase the heat to medium–high and add the cheese slices to
the pan. Fry for a few minutes on both sides, to a light golden
brown. Pour the vinegar over the cheese and add the oregano
and pepper. Cover the pan and leave on the heat for just a few
minutes. Serve the cheese immediately with some crusty
bread – it must be served very hot.
Serves 4

Carciofi *Ripieni*

STUFFED ARTICHOKES

4 young artichokes

½ organic lemon

125 ml (4 fl oz) virgin olive oil

4 anchovy fillets in oil, drained

2 cloves garlic, crushed

50 g (2 oz) fresh breadcrumbs

½ bunch Italian flat-leaf parsley, finely chopped

20 g (¾ oz) capers in brine, drained

50 g (2 oz) freshly grated pecorino

salt and pepper

150 ml (5 fl oz) dry white wine

Preheat the oven to 180°C (350°F).

To prepare the artichokes, trim the stalks, leaving around 2 cm (¾ in). Remove the tough outer leaves and cut a third off the tops of the artichokes. Hold the artichokes by the stems and bang them briefly on the kitchen counter so that they open to expose the inner hairy choke (if the artichokes are very young there may be no choke at all). With a sharp knife, remove the choke and quickly rub the cut surfaces with lemon to stop them discolouring.

Heat half the oil in a frying pan. Add the anchovies and garlic and fry over a gentle heat. Add the breadcrumbs and cook for a few more minutes, stirring. Be careful not to let the mixture burn. Add the parsley and capers and stir for another 3 minutes. Mix the grated cheese in thoroughly and take the pan off the heat. Leave to cool slightly then taste and season.

With your fingers, gently open up the artichokes and fill the centres with the stuffing. Try to push some of the stuffing in between the leaves.

Lightly butter an ovenproof dish. Arrange the artichokes in the dish and drizzle the remaining olive oil over them. Bake for 20 minutes. Pour the wine over the artichokes and return to the oven for another 20 minutes until they are deliciously crunchy. The artichokes are best eaten at room temperature.

Serves 4

Crostata
DI AMARETTI E *Cioccolato*
AMARETTI AND CHOCOLATE TART

PASTRY

250 g (9 oz) self-raising flour

120 g (4 oz) caster
(superfine) sugar

2 organic egg yolks

120 g (4 oz) unsalted butter
at room temperature

pinch of salt

FILLING

4 organic egg whites

75 g (2½ oz) bitter
chocolate, finely chopped

75 g (2½ oz) almonds,
toasted and finely chopped

75 g (2½ oz) amaretti
biscuits, finely chopped

icing (confectioner's)
sugar for dusting (optional)

To make the pastry, put all the ingredients into a food processor and pulse until the dough is just amalgamated. Roll it into a ball and place it in the refrigerator to rest for an hour.

Preheat the oven to 180°C (350°F) and butter a 23 cm (9 in) springform cake tin.

Roll the pastry out on a lightly floured work surface then lift it into the prepared tin so the pastry comes up the sides.

To make the filling, beat the egg whites until they form stiff peaks, but are not dry. Fold in the chocolate, almonds and amaretti. Pour the filling into the pastry shell and bake for around 35 minutes.

Remove from the oven. Release the sides of the tin and remove the tart. Leave to cool completely and serve dusted with icing sugar, if you like.

Serves 6

The Island of *Ortigia*

THE CITY OF SYRACUSE IS TO THE EAST OF SICILY WHAT PALERMO IS TO THE west. It is the site of some great events in history. It was founded by Greek settlers in the eighth century BC and grew to become one of the most powerful cities in their Empire, famous throughout the ancient Greek world. Syracuse boasts Archimedes as an early citizen and later it was home to a passing parade of conquerors, who have all left their mark on this World Heritage Site.

Just offshore from Syracuse, separated from the mainland by a hundred-metre-long bridge, is the island of Ortigia, famous today for its medieval and baroque buildings. Ortigia is small, no more than a few kilometres in circumference, and it has an atmosphere all of its own. It has many of the elements I love about a town: it is not too large, the buildings are beautiful, there is only limited access for cars, and it has an exceptional produce market and very good restaurants. On top of all that, Ortigia has a great setting on the sea with a working port. Every time I go there I enjoy it immensely.

Ortigia is a very charming city. Its principal buildings, and many others, have been carefully maintained or restored and the fact that it is essentially a pedestrian

Opposite: The island of Ortigia from the water

Above: The fortress of Miniace (top left) on the headland of Ortigia

city gives it a special character that it shares with places like Venice. As we were there in spring, we discovered that the city holds a competition called 'Ortigia in Fiore' (Ortigia in Flower) for the best gardens or floral displays. Everywhere we looked there were window boxes in bloom and balconies and small entrances set out with pots of flowering shrubs or plants – mini gardens that looked wonderful, and also told us that the inhabitants of this city are very proud of it.

The way to see Ortigia, to really get the feel of the place, is to walk. In a few hours you can see most of the island. On our first evening in Ortigia we decided to reacquaint ourselves with some of its delights. We began with a leisurely stroll along the quay that stretches the full length of the port and is lined with grand buildings. A block inland we found ourselves in a maze of streets and medieval buildings. Some laneways are so narrow, particularly in the old Jewish quarter, that you can stand with your arms outstretched and touch the buildings on both sides. In the centre of the island there is a generous piazza, which is where you'll find the most elaborate buildings on the island – the cathedral, the town hall, a bishop's palace and another church. The buildings and the flagstones of the piazza are all made from a pale local

stone that gives the overall picture a pleasing uniformity. A few citrus trees poke their tips over the wall of a high garden overlooking the piazza.

After our walk, we sat at an outdoor caffé to enjoy the scene, drink a strong espresso and sample a lemon sorbet that was deliciously sharp (white outside and the palest green inside). It was early evening and the passegiata was in full swing. In front of us was a slow parade of people of all ages keen on seeing and being seen. I watched a male pigeon dragging around a huge twig between the tables as it chased a female, as if to say, 'Look at the nest I could build you!' In a performance that mirrored the pigeon, a number of the local lads were 'dragging their own twigs' around in front of the local girls, who were pretending not to notice.

Walking back from the piazza I stopped in front of a recommended restaurant to read the menu. Noticing that an older man was watching us with interest, I asked him, 'Do you eat well here?' He replied, 'Well the portions are small, the food's not very good and it's expensive!' After that information I asked him where he would choose to eat and he named a restaurant not far away. Outside the second restaurant was another man, so I asked him, 'Do you eat well here?' 'That depends,'

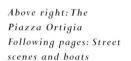

Above right: The Piazza Ortigia
Following pages: Street scenes and boats

167

he replied. 'On what?' we asked. 'On me, I'm the owner and the chef.' Naturally we decided to stay, and enjoyed one of those memorable dinners where you order nothing and the food and wine just arrive. The restaurant was the Pan-ta-rei, and the chef, Donato Tetto.

In fact we ate memorably well a number of times in Ortigia. At one lunch we ordered an insalata caprese (mozzarella and tomatoes) and the plate arrived with three small balls of the freshest and most beautifully made mozzarella, sliced tomatoes still a little green (Sicilians prefer their tomatoes with 'green shoulders') and a great local olive oil. The waiter apologised to us heartily, 'You will have to wait five minutes because the bread is still baking.' Wonderful bread it was too, made from yellow grano duro flour. The simplest of meals, but perfection of a sort.

On another day, we enjoyed a delicious lunch of various seafood plates. Through the restaurant windows we could see the fishing boats unloading their catch on the quay. In the restaurant the very same produce was then laid out on ice in a grand display. Everyone who came in headed immediately to view the display and made their choices.

In fact one of the great joys of Ortigia is the quality and freshness of its produce. The local market is everything you hope for and we made a point of visiting it during our visit. It is located on a wide street with the ruins of the old Roman forum at one end and the Porto Piccolo with the sea beyond at the other.

We noticed that some of the produce was different from what we had seen in Palermo. There were mounds of local lemons that are eaten green (inland from Syracuse is a great citrus-growing area), mandarins, mini prickly pears, capers and mounds of strattu (tomato concentrate). Another local speciality was dried tomatoes grown in the sand dunes near Pachino in the south – they acquire a naturally salty flavour that is most unusual.

There were lots of local cheeses including some unusual lightly cooked mozzarella and some tricotta (twice-baked ricotta). The cheese vendor was full of local wisdom: 'It's easier to make cheese than children,' he said. 'With cheese you can see right away whether it's turned out well.'

Maybe it's the view of the Porto Piccolo down the street or the awareness that Ortigia is an island, but for me the stars of the market were the fishmongers.

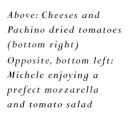

Above: Cheeses and Pachino dried tomatoes (bottom right) Opposite, bottom left: Michele enjoying a prefect mozzarella and tomato salad

In Palermo in springtime the pride of place on the marble counters are great red slabs of tuna. In Ortigia the swordfish reigns supreme. The pale flesh of the swordfish does not have the impact of tuna, so it marks its presence with a long sword jutting from its head towards the sky. Swordfish are caught just out to sea from Ortigia, in the Straits of Messina between Sicily and the mainland, and spring is the season for the catch. Around the swordfish were arranged the lesser creatures of the sea (all delicious) – baby calamari, baby octopus, mussels, sea urchins and lots of local fish.

Chatting to the vendor at one fish stall he told me a classic migrant's tale (markets are all about the chat as well as the produce) of his cousin, who had gone to Australia to start a small sheep farm outside Melbourne. 'It didn't work out,' he said. 'The sheep all died because they were poisoned by the gold under the soil.' It has been one hundred and fifty years since the gold-rush days in Melbourne but the legend lives on in Ortigia!

The Ortigia market has the best spice and herb store I saw in the whole of Sicily. On a corner site in the middle of the market, Antonio Drago presides over an Aladdin's cave of sacks, boxes, jars and tins that give off the most extraordinary

MISWAK ARAK

SCORZE ARANCIA

ZENZERO CANDITO

CAPER CUCUMBER

T... VE...

AROMI per CARNE

UVA PASSITA

MISTO SPAGHETTI CAMPAGNOLA

CAPPERI PANTELLERIA

LE OLIVE COME UNA VOLTA....
ALLA CONTADINA

SALAMOIA - ANETO - AGLIO
LIMONE - PEPERONCINO
....E BASTA !

SALAMOIA · ANETO · AGLIO
LIMONE · PEPERONC...

BORLOTTI FAGIOLA PASTA

MINESTRONE di LEGUMI - ORZO PE...

FIENO GRECO

SENAPE MOSTARDA GIALLA

CARVI KÜMMEL

CREN = RAFANO

PAPRIKA FORTE

*Above: The Ortigia quay
lined by pleached figs*

aromas. He claims to have every spice you can think of and is full of stories about all the good things he sells. From Antonio we learnt that carob nuts were used to weigh gold because they were of uniform weight. In fact the carat, the old unit of measurement for gold, comes from the word carob. He is a one-man encyclopedia of local food knowledge.

I have always believed that the best way to see island cities is from the water. In some, the buildings and houses face out to the sea to maximise the views. But in many older island cities you find the buildings turn inwards for protection, and Ortigia is one of these. The guide books tell you it has been destroyed and rebuilt seven times, so you can understand why the inhabitants felt they needed protection.

Ortigia is a marvellous sight from the sea. The main quay is lined by a row of pleached fig trees and rising behind them, the classical stone facades. In the centre of the foreshore is a famous freshwater spring, surrounded by papyrus. A place of beauty and mystery, it was also strategically important in times when the island was under siege. On the headland stands the fortress of Miniace, built by Frederick Barbarossa, the same king who was the ancestor of the Conte Federico in Palermo.

From the water you can see a small low gate in the wall that leads to a rock shelf and a shallow pool, obviously man-made. Local legend has it that this is where Frederick would come to bathe with his 'ancelle' (girlfriends). In those days people couldn't swim, so it must have been considered the height of luxury for him to have his own private wading pool.

On our last evening in Ortigia we ate at a restaurant on a long, high promenade looking back over the water towards the setting sun. Often in places like this you are disappointed – they are too touristy or the splendid view means the restaurant thinks it can get away with serving ordinary food at high prices. Neither was true in this case and the whole experience encapsulated Ortigia at its best.

In thinking about recipes that best capture the spirit of Ortigia, my first choice is Caponatina, a vegetable dish of capsicums, eggplants, tomatoes and onions. There is a local saying that every Sicilian woman knows how to make caponatina – it is passed on to her 'con il latte della Mamma' (from her mother's milk). The classic caponatina is an agro–dolce dish that uses both vinegar and sugar. Every restaurant (and every family) seems to make it differently, but they all make it. It is one of the

Above, left: Church in the Piazza Ortigia

signature dishes of Sicilian cooking. If you taste it, I think you will see what all the fuss is about.

Fave con pecorino are baby broad beans drizzled with oil and served with shavings of pecorino. They are often served as a stuzzichino – a delectable nibble to accompany your aperitivi.

Another vegetable dish, Radicchio alla Griglia, is simplicity itself but really delicious. The brightly coloured and rather bitter radicchio leaves are grilled and dressed with nothing but oil and salt.

Porri e Patate al Forno (leek and potato gratin) is a dish I think you will really enjoy. Layers of leeks and potatoes are dressed with cream, rosemary and garlic and then baked. It is eaten on its own or as an accompaniment to fish or meat.

I have to include a recipe for Ortigia's famous swordfish and I have chosen a simple dish of swordfish grilled with a Salmoriglio sauce. This is an oil and lemon emulsion, flavoured with oregano thought to date from the time of the Greeks, and it goes wonderfully well with the fish.

For dessert I've chosen Torta di Noci (walnut cake), which is made using ricotta, walnuts and breadcrumbs, a very Sicilian combination.

Caponatina

1 kg (2 lb 3 oz) small, young eggplants

250–375 ml (8½–12 fl oz) virgin olive oil

2 red capsicums (bell peppers), thinly sliced

1 large Spanish onion, sliced

2–3 celery stalks, sliced

2 carrots, diced

10 anchovy fillets in oil, drained

250 g (9 oz) tomato concentrate

400 g (14 oz) canned Italian tomatoes

75 ml (2½ fl oz) red-wine vinegar

1 tablespoon sugar

70 g (2½ oz) pitted green olives

2 tablespoons pine nuts, lightly toasted

1 large handful Italian flat-leaf parsley, chopped

salt and pepper

1 large handful fresh basil leaves, chopped

If you use small, young eggplants you do not need to salt them to draw out the bitterness.

Cut the eggplants into 2 cm (¾ in) cubes.

Heat 200 ml (7 fl oz) of olive oil in a large saucepan. Fry the eggplant cubes in batches until they are pale gold all over. Remove from the pan with a slotted spoon and drain on kitchen paper.

If needed add more oil and fry the capsicum slices until they are soft. Remove from the pan and drain on kitchen paper. Add a little more oil to the pan and fry the onion, celery and carrots until soft, but not coloured. Add the anchovies and tomato concentrate and cook for 5–10 minutes, until the mixture turns a rich, dark red. Add the canned tomatoes and cook for 15 minutes over a low heat, stirring from time to time. Stir in the vinegar and sugar and cook for 10 minutes. Add the olives, pine nuts and parsley, together with the eggplant and capsicum. Cook for 10 more minutes then remove from the heat and leave to cool.

Just before serving, taste and adjust the seasoning to your liking then stir in the basil. Serve at room temperature or cold.

Serves 6

Fave
<small>CON</small> *Pecorino*

BROAD BEANS WITH PECORINO

**400 g (14 oz) very
young broad beans**

200 g (7 oz) pecorino

**60 ml (2 fl oz) good-quality
virgin olive oil**

sea salt flakes

*This is a dish that is best made in spring, when the broad beans
are fresh and young. Eat them as a pre-starter, with a nice glass
of light rosé, as you are waiting for your meal to arrive.*

Pop the bread beans out of their pods. If they are very young
there is no need to blanch and peel them. Shave the pecorino
over the beans and drizzle with olive oil. Sprinkle
with salt and serve.

Serves 4

Radicchio
ALLA *Griglia*
GRILLED RADICCHIO

½ young radicchio per person
virgin olive oil
salt flakes
freshly ground black pepper

This very simple dish is a delicious accompaniment to grilled fish or meat, and equally good served as part of an antipasto.

Preheat a barbecue or griddle plate to high.

Cut the radicchio into quarter-wedges and drizzle with olive oil. Grill or barbecue for a few minutes until the radicchio starts to colour.

Transfer to a serving dish and drizzle with a little more oil.

Sprinkle with salt and pepper and serve.

Porri

E PATATE *al Forno*

LEEK AND POTATO GRATIN

50 g (2 oz) unsalted butter

3 tablespoons virgin olive oil

6 young leeks, trimmed
and sliced

3 cloves garlic, thinly sliced

1 kg (2 lb 3 oz) waxy potatoes
(desirée or King Edward),
sliced very thinly

350 ml (12 fl oz) cream

2 fresh rosemary sprigs,
stalks discarded

salt and pepper

Preheat the oven to 200°C (400°F).

Heat the butter and oil in a large saucepan. Add the leeks and garlic, cover the pan and sweat over a low heat for 15 minutes, stirring from time to time. The leeks should be soft and sweet. Butter an ovenproof dish and arrange a layer of sliced potatoes over the base. Cover with some of the leeks, then pour on some cream and sprinkle with some of the rosemary and salt and pepper. Continue layering until all the ingredients are used up. Finish with a layer of potatoes, covered with cream, and sprinkled with rosemary, salt and pepper.

Transfer to the oven and bake for around 35 minutes until the top is golden.

Serves 6

Pesce

SPADA AL *Salmoriglio*

GRILLED & SWORDFISH
WITH SALMORIGLIO SAUCE

SALMORIGLIO SAUCE

120 ml (4 fl oz) virgin olive oil

60 ml (2 fl oz) warm water

juice of 1 organic lemon

2 cloves garlic, very finely
chopped

1 tablespoon finely chopped
fresh oregano

1 tablespoon finely chopped
fresh Italian flat-leaf parsley

1 small red chilli, partially
seeded and very finely chopped
(optional)

4 x 150 g (5 oz) slices of
swordfish (about
1 cm (½ in) thick)

1 tablespoon virgin olive oil

salt flakes and pepper

*Oregano and garlic are two very traditional flavourings in
Sicilian cooking. They were introduced by the Greeks and
you'll find them featuring in all sorts of grilled dishes.*
Preheat your grill to high.

To prepare the sauce, whisk the oil in a mixing bowl and
very slowly add the warm water and lemon juice, whisking
continuously to form an emulsion. Add the garlic, herbs and
chilli (if using).

Pat the swordfish slices dry with kitchen paper and rub them
all over with oil. Grill for around 2 minutes on each side.
Remove the fish from the grill and season with salt and pepper.
Serve straight away, with the sauce spooned over the fish.
Alternatively, serve the sauce on the side in a warm jug.

Serves 4

Torta
DI *Noci*
WALNUT CAKE

180 g (6 oz) fresh breadcrumbs

200 g (7 oz) walnuts, lightly toasted

300 g (10½ oz) caster (superfine) sugar

100 g (3½ oz) unsalted butter at room temperature

6 organic eggs, separated

200 g (7 oz) fresh ricotta

1 teaspoon ground cinnamon

½ teaspoon ground cloves

grated zest of 1 organic lemon

pinch of salt

1 tablespoon icing (confectioner's) sugar for decoration

This cake uses breadcrumbs and ground walnuts instead of flour. It is a very light but fragrant cake, ideally eaten with tea in the afternoon.

Preheat the oven to 190°C (375°F).

Butter the sides of a 23 cm (9 in) cake tin and line the base with greaseproof paper. Sprinkle ¼ cup of the breadcrumbs onto the sides of the cake tin, pressing them in gently.

Combine the walnuts with half the sugar in a food processor and pulse until you have a fine, flour-like consistency.

In an electric mixer, beat the rest of the sugar with the butter until very light and fluffy. Add the egg yolks, one at a time, and continue beating until they are all incorporated and the mixture is light and airy. Fold in the ground walnut mixture, ricotta, spices, lemon zest and salt.

In a separate bowl, whisk the egg whites to stiff peaks. Fold into the cake batter then pour into the cake tin. Transfer to the oven and bake for 35–40 minutes.

Remove from the oven, release the sides of the tin and remove the cake. Leave to cool completely then place the cake on a serving plate and dust with icing sugar.

Serves 8

Mount Etna

LIFE ON THE *Edge*

Opposite: Mt Etna volcano with smoke from its top

THE LANDSCAPE IN THE TOP NORTHEASTERN CORNER OF SICILY IS DOMINATED by the brooding presence of Mount Etna. At more than 3300 metres in height, with a snow cap much of the year, Etna is a striking outline on the skyline. The most remarkable thing about Etna however is not its height but the fact it is a live volcano. By daylight wisps of smoke can be seen hovering above the summit or, more worryingly, coming out of the sides of the mountain. By night the spectacle is compelling. High up on the black mountain slopes, lava spills down like a red glove. Etna is alive and dangerous. Volcanologists and local folklore say that these tiny eruptions release pressure and ensure the mountain does not explode, but this is only an educated guess, or maybe wishful thinking.

While Etna threatens, she also gives. The volcanic soils and benign micro-climate around the mountain make the area particularly fertile and productive. Fruits, vines and nuts grow in abundance and are renowned for their quality. The locals call this 'Etna Dolce' — Sweet Etna. Fishermen believe Etna Dolce extends even to the local seafood. Beneath the sea different varieties of seaweeds and grasses grow on the lava rock. These, in turn, make the fish who feed on them taste better.

SAN DOMENICO
PALACE HOTEL
TAORMINA

Above: Taormina at dusk

While the riches of Etna Dolce continue to attract more people closer to the mountain, the dangers are real. This is life on the edge.

Our first stop in the Etna region was the famous beauty spot of Taormina. Situated on a steep site with the sea below and Etna to the south, the town has breathtaking views. About one hundred and fifty years ago it was 'discovered' by a rather Bohemian group of well-off northern Europeans who built villas there for the summer or as a year-round escape. The old villas and their gardens are still there, although most have been converted into hotels to cater for the hoards of tourists who visit. While undeniably scenic, I think the pressures of tourism dominate the town.

My favourite moment in Taormina was sitting on the terrace of the San Domenico Hotel enjoying an aperitivo as the sun went down. The San Domenico was once a monastery, and the grand facade is swathed with masses of purple and red bougainvillea, as if in sympathy with the cardinals and bishops from its past. The gardens below the terrace are beautifully laid out and richly planted. A cliff drops to the sea and to your right is a long walkway framed at its end by Norfolk Island

Above: The garden at the San Domenico Hotel, Taormina

pines. In the centre of this frame is Etna, its plume of smoke wisping against the sky. At such moments you understand the attraction of Taormina to the people who came and never left.

The northern slopes of Etna run down to generous open valleys and this is an area of intense cultivation. We were we staying at the Borgo San Nicolao Agriturismo, a working farm in the valley run by the La Mancusa family. On the farm, fruit trees, olives and vines grow in ordered profusion over a terraced landscape. One brother, Francesco, runs the farm and another brother, Santo, is a cheese maker (see him at his craft on page 149). At the top of the property is an old stone building – a nevaia, or snow house. In the olden days, snow was brought down from the mountain in winter and stored beneath layers of bracken and salt for sale in summer. The remarkable thing about the La Mancusa's farm is that it can be run almost entirely on organic practices. It seems that the lava has an extraordinary effect on the soil and air, so that most crops require no chemical treatments, and just a little care. The olives, for instance, don't suffer from olive fly – the problem that the Titone Olive Grove overcame only with great difficulty.

*Above and opposite:
The Passopisciaro
vineyard, Mt Etna;
wine maker Vincenzo
Lo Mauro (below)*

Higher up the mountain, at the edge of the national park, you can see new plantings of vines. Wine from Etna – Etna DOC – is gaining a reputation for innovation and quality. The black lava soils and the elevation – vineyards grow up to 1000 metres – give new winemakers the chance to produce wines with strong local characteristics. We visited one such vineyard, high on the mountain. The Passopisciaro vineyard is being developed by Andrea Franchetti, a Tuscan wine producer who is attracted to the special possibilities of the area.

On our visit, we learned that Passopisciaro had been producing wine until a lava flow came to the boundary of the property in 1943 and stopped production. We were fascinated to look at a wine map of the area. It showed the various vineyards and their elevations, but it also showed the outlines and dates of lava flows. You can see flows down to 800 metres in 1911, and down to 800–1000 metres in 1943 and 1947.

Like the produce from the Borgo San Nicolao farm in the valley below, Passopisciaro vines need fewer chemical treatments over a season – five or six compared to perhaps twenty in the average Piemonte vineyard. The elevation also means a big difference between day and night time temperatures (about 12°C), leading to

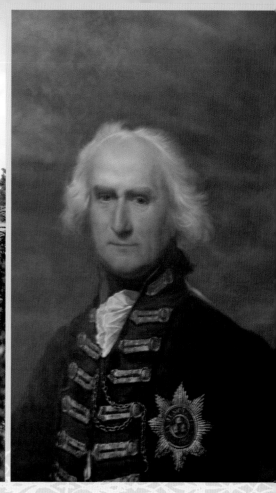

Above and opposite: Views of the house and garden of Nelson's ancestral seat in Maniace

slower maturity, later picking and greater flavour. The development of sophisticated wine making high on Etna is something quite new, and I suspect we will be hearing a lot more about it in the future.

Travelling west around the flanks of Etna is the town of Bronte, the centre for the cultivation of pistachio nuts, a popular ingredient in local cooking. Before I visited the town, I wanted to visit the ancestral seat of the dukes of Bronte in the nearby valley. This is the house that was given to Lord Nelson by a grateful King of Naples after Nelson defeated Napoleon at sea. Nelson was made Duke of Bronte, given an old abbey in the village of Maniace and 16,000 hectares of land – a vast estate. Nelson's descendants turned the abbey into a suitably grand house and lived there on and off until they relinquished ownership in the 1980s. Castello Nelson is a collection of stone buildings around two large courtyards. The main house is long rather than wide, and looks onto a garden that, in its day, was famous throughout Europe. Although the garden has been rather neglected, enough trees and walls remain to see what it would once have been in its heyday. On a distant hillside, once part of the estate, you can see cypresses planted in the form of the

ducal coronet, only some of the trees have died so the crown has slipped somewhat. The interiors of the house are well preserved with lots of Nelson memorabilia and large paintings of naval battles. With painted tiles on the floors and furniture from England and Italy, it is a comfortable mix between a Sicilian palazzo and an English country house.

After visiting Castello Nelson, we continued on to the town of Bronte. Built of black lava stone and sprawling in a disordered way over a slope, it is rather an unlovely spot. However it does have one exceptional food venue, the Pasticcerria Conti Gallenti. We discovered it, as you often find the best places, by asking someone in the street where we could try the best ice cream.

Here I have a confession to make. The purpose of our visit was to taste pistachio ice cream – this is after all the pistachio centre of Sicily – but I have a weakness for nocciola (hazelnut) ice cream, and I must try it wherever I go. I have to say it was the best nocciola I have ever tasted, and that's saying something!

My husband Michele and Simon, our photographer, sampled the pistachio ice cream, which was a wonderful pale green colour, nutty and delicious. They also

Above: Pistachio ice cream in a brioche (left) and my nocciola (right) at Pasticceria Conti Galenti

199

*Above: St Agatha
(bottom left) and the
cathedral (bottom
right), Catania*

tasted a locally created drink called Iceburg, which is a small scoop of sharp lemon granita served in a long glass with sparkling mineral water. It is very refreshing.

As you leave Bronte you can see pistachio nuts growing on the hillside. The ground is all rough black lava, sharp and very broken-up, and the pistachio trees grow in the cracks and crevices. They are small trees, more like a large bush, and look a little like a very untidy and straggly fig tree. The combination of the harsh terrain and scrappy vegetation is not very aesthetically pleasing, but the conditions produce a pistachio nut with high oil content and lots of flavour.

Our tour of Mount Etna finished in the provincial capital, Catania. Etna has threatened Catania through most of its history. Every year the patron saint of the city, Saint Agatha, is taken from her sanctuary in the cathedral and paraded in an elaborate procession to the city gates. If there were an eruption, Saint Agatha would be called on to stop it.

Catania is a rather somber and untidy city, built from black lava stone, sometimes banded with white. The Duomo (cathedral) is a very grand building with a marvellous interior. If you stand inside the cathedral and look back out the main

Above: Mt Etna and its surrounding 'Etna Dolce' countryside

door, past the huge low-hanging banners, you can see the piazza, and beyond it the long stretch of Via Etna heading straight towards the mountain. In the nearby pasticceria they sell a local specialty – small marzipan-covered cakes in the shape of breasts, complete with nipples. These represent Saint Agatha, whose breasts were cut off when she was martyred. It's a grim story and a rather bizarre way to remember it, but it suits the mood of the city.

As you would expect, the food you eat around Etna Dolce is very good indeed.

We had a number of exceptional dinners at Borgo San Nicolao where the food was good country food, 'molto tipico'. An antipasto selection of local cheeses and hams would be followed by a choice of pasta dishes and then some meat or fish. To finish the meal, we would be offered a home-made liqueur as a digestivo. I have already given the recipe for Pasta al Borgo San Nicolao (page 118), so here I am including the recipe for Liquore di Alloro, a liqueur made from bay leaves that we drank there.

I have chosen two recipes that are ideal to serve with aperitivi. First there is Giardiniera (pickled vegetables) and secondly, Olive Verdi Siciliane (pickled green olives). Both these nibbles have quite a sharp, spicy flavour.

Another good snack to eat with aperitivi is Sfincione, a local pizza. And it also makes a tasty light meal.

Eggplants are widely used in Sicily and I'm including a recipe for Melanzane alla Parmigiana, a baked eggplant dish. You will find a version of this dish on many Sicilian restaurant menus as it is something of a classic.

Involtini di Agnello (rolled lamb with asparagus) is a country dish to eat when you are celebrating. If you taste it you will see why these rolls are made for special occasions.

You can argue whether sorbets and granitas were first created from snow from Mount Vesuvius (near Naples) or Mount Etna. Whatever your view, the area around Mount Etna has always been famous for its flavoured ices made from snow. The ice was traditionally taken from the snow house, shaved and added to sweet, flavoured syrups. I have included three wonderful granita recipes: Granita al Caffé (coffee granita), al Gelso (mulberry) and the classic al Limone (lemon).

Finally, there is a recipe using pistachio nuts to make Mazaresi, which are small pistachio cakes.

Opposite: The bay below Taormina

Liquore
AL *Alloro*
BAY LEAF LIQUEUR

40 fresh bay leaves
½ bottle vodka
500 g (1 lb 2 oz) caster sugar
200 ml (7 fl oz) water
zest of 1 large organic lemon
(make sure you use only
the yellow zest as the white
pith is bitter)

This liqueur is a great digestive to enjoy after a big dinner!
Combine the bay leaves and vodka in a sealed glass jar and leave
them to infuse for 15 days.
After the 15 days, add the sugar, water and lemon zest and leave
in a cool, dark place for a minimum of 2 months. Shake the jar
from time to time until all the sugar has dissolved.
Strain before drinking.
Makes around 1 litre (2 pints) liqueur

Thé
ALL' *Alloro*
BAY LEAF TEA

2 fresh bay leaves per person
1 wide strip of organic
lemon zest per person
sugar

*This is a lovely fragrant tea that makes a change from the
usual herbal selection. It's perfect as an after-dinner digestive.*
Place the ingredients in a teapot or in individual cups, adding
sugar to taste.
Pour on boiling water and allow to steep for 3–4 minutes
before drinking.

Giardiniera
PICKLED VEGETABLES

PICKLING LIQUID

800 ml (26 fl oz) good-quality
white-wine vinegar

800 ml (26 fl oz) water

2 tablespoons honey

6 juniper berries

6 cloves

10 peppercorns

2 small red chillies

3 fresh bay leaves

8 very small pearl onions

4 small carrots, cut into
4 cm (½ in) sticks

4 celery stalks (the young,
light-green ones), cut
into 4 cm (½ in) sticks

½ small cauliflower,
broken up into small florets

200 g (7 oz) young beans,
tops and tails trimmed

10 cloves garlic, peeled

Place all the pickling liquid ingredients in a large non-reactive saucepan. Bring to the boil, then cover the pan and simmer gently for 15 minutes.

Add the onions to the pan and simmer for 5 minutes. Add the remaining ingredients and when the liquid returns to the boil, remove the pan from the heat.

Sterilise a 2 litre (4 pint) glass jar or 2 x 1 litre (2 pint) jars. Spoon the vegetables into the sterilised jar, and pour in enough of the pickling liquid to cover them completely. Seal and allow to cool. Refrigerate for 2 days before eating. Once opened, the giardiniera will keep up to 2 months in the refrigerator.

Makes a 2 litre (4 pint) jar

Olive

VERDI *Siciliane*

PICKLED GREEN OLIVES

2 kg (4 lb 6 oz) fresh
green olives

1 kg (2 lb 3 oz) salt

3–4 carrots, cut into
2 cm (½ in) lengths

3–4 young celery stalks, cut
into 2 cm (½ in) lengths

3 fresh bay leaves

3 wild fennel
(or fresh dill) sprigs

2 small red chillies

4 cloves garlic

1 litre (2 pints)
white-wine vinegar

1 litre (2 pints) virgin olive oil

With a sharp knife, make a cut in each olive. Place them in a container large enough to hold them loosely. Add two big handfuls of salt and cover with cold water. Sit a plate on top of the olives to keep them submerged in the water. Leave for 24 hours.

The following day, drain the olives and return them to the container. Repeat the soaking process in fresh water and with more salt. Repeat daily until the olives have lost their bitterness, which will take up to 18 days.

Drain the olives and return them to the container. Add the vegetables, herbs, chillies and garlic and cover with vinegar. Leave overnight.

The following day, drain off the vinegar then arrange all the ingredients on a tray and put out in the sun to dry for 5 hours, turning from time to time to ensure everything dries evenly. Sterilise a 2 litre (4 pint) glass jar or 2 x 1 litre (2 pint) jars. Spoon the dried ingredients into the sterilised jar and pour in enough olive oil to cover them completely. Shake the jar a few times to make sure the oil covers everything evenly. Leave in a cool dark place for at least a week before eating.

Makes around 2–2½ kg (4 lb 4 oz – 5 lb 5 oz)

Sfincione

PIZZA WITH ANCHOVIES
AND CACIOCAVALLO

PIZZA DOUGH

600 g (1 lb 5 oz) unbleached plain flour (preferably Italian 'Tipo 00')

2 teaspoons salt

1 tablespoon granulated yeast

3 tablespoons extra-virgin olive oil

around 375–500 ml (12–17 fl oz) warm water

TOPPING

90–120 ml (3–4 fl oz) virgin olive oil

2 large Spanish onions, finely sliced

20 anchovy fillets in oil, drained and roughly broken up

20 pitted black olives

200 g (7 oz) Caciocavallo or pecorino, thinly sliced

2 tablespoons fresh breadcrumbs

2 tablespoons fresh oregano, chopped

salt flakes and pepper

Sfincione is a well-seasoned pizza that can be eaten with aperitivi, as a first course or even as a light main course.

To make the pizza dough, combine all the ingredients in a large mixing bowl. Turn onto a work surface and knead until it becomes smooth, shiny and elastic. If it looks too dry, add a little more water. If it looks too wet, add a little more flour. Shape into a ball and rub with a little oil. Leave in a warm place, covered with a tea towel, for about an hour.

Preheat the oven to 220°C (430°F).

Heat around 2 tablespoons of the oil in a large frying pan and add the onions. Fry for 5 minutes or until soft and translucent.

Oil a 30 x 40 cm (12 x 16 in) oven tray. Roll the pizza dough out and lift it onto the tray. Use your fingers to push it into the corners and to make indentations over the surface. Brush generously with olive oil. Spread the onions over the pizza base, followed by the anchovies, olives, cheese, breadcrumbs and oregano. Drizzle on the remaining oil and sprinkle with a few salt flakes and pepper. Be lenient with the salt as the anchovies and olives are already salty.

Bake in the oven for 20 minutes.

Serves 4–6

Involtini

DI *Agnello*

ROLLED LAMB WITH ASPARAGUS

800–900 g (1 lb 12 oz – 2 lb)
lamb backstraps (loins)

salt and pepper

2 fresh fior di latte (cow's milk
mozzarella) balls

24 anchovy fillets in
oil, drained

2 bunches young asparagus

2 rosemary sprigs,
stalks discarded

unbleached plain flour
for dusting

100 g (3½ oz) unsalted butter

60 ml (2 fl oz) virgin olive oil

150 ml (5 fl oz) dry Marsala

Cut each lamb backstrap in half, then slice it lengthwise into thirds (you will have 6 slices per backstrap). With a meat mallet, pound the lamb slices as thinly as you can into rectangles. Pat them dry on kitchen paper and season lightly (remember that the anchovies are salty).

Lay the lamb slices out on your work surface with the long edges facing you. Cut the fior di latte into very thin slices and place 1 slice on top of each piece of lamb – it should cover about a third of the lamb slice. Arrange 1 anchovy and 2 asparagus spears crosswise on top of the cheese and sprinkle with a few rosemary leaves. Roll the lamb tightly around the filling and secure with a toothpick or string. Dust the involtini in flour, shaking off any excess.

In a large frying pan, fry the involtini in batches in the butter and oil with the rest of the rosemary. Turn them so they colour evenly. Transfer to a warmed dish.

Once the involtini are all cooked, add the Marsala to the pan and cook for a few minutes, scraping up any bits from the base of the pan. Return the involtini to the pan and roll them around in the sauce. Lower the heat and cover the pan. Cook gently for about 10 minutes, adding a little more Marsala or water if it seems too dry. Serve hot from the pan.

Serves 6

Melanzane

ALLA *Parmigiana*
BAKED EGGPLANT

TOMATO SAUCE

50 g (2 oz) unsalted butter

2 tablespoons virgin olive oil

1 large Spanish onion, sliced

3 cloves garlic, finely chopped

4–5 fresh sage leaves

2 fresh bay leaves

20 anchovy fillets

250 g (9 oz) tomato concentrate

800 g (1 lb 12 oz) canned
Italian tomatoes

handful fresh basil leaves,
roughly chopped

5–6 small eggplants

600 ml (20 fl oz)
peanut oil for frying

3 large mozzarella balls,
broken into small pieces

salt and pepper

100 g (3½ oz) freshly
grated Parmiggiano,
plus 200 g (7 oz) to serve

70 g (2½ oz) unsalted butter

This popular dish is best eaten hot, but can also be eaten at room temperature.

To make the sauce, heat the butter and oil in a medium-sized saucepan. Add the onion and garlic and fry gently until soft and translucent. Add the sage, bay leaves, anchovies and tomato concentrate and cook for around 10 minutes, until the mixture turns a rich, dark red. Add the tomatoes and cook for 10 minutes over a low heat, stirring from time to time. Remove from the heat and stir in the basil.

Preheat the oven to 200°C (400°F).

Cut the eggplants lengthwise into 5 mm (¼ in) slices and pat dry on kitchen paper. Heat the oil in a large frying pan. When it is hot, fry the eggplant slices in batches until golden, turning so they colour evenly. Remove from the pan and drain on kitchen paper.

Butter a 25 x 35 cm (10 x 14 in) ovenproof dish. Arrange a layer of eggplant slices over the base of the dish, covering it completely. Spread 4–5 tablespoons tomato sauce over the eggplant and top with pieces of mozarella. Add a little salt and pepper then sprinkle on 1–2 tablespoons grated Parmiggiano. Continue layering the ingredients, finishing with a layer of tomato sauce. Dot the surface evenly with pieces of butter then bake in the oven for around 20 minutes, or until golden. Serve at the table with the remaining Parmiggiano.

Serves 6

Granita

AL *Caffè*

COFFEE GRANITA

125 g (4 oz) caster
(superfine) sugar

200 ml (7 fl oz) very
strong espresso coffee

200 ml (7 fl oz) water

whipped cream to serve

Dissolve the sugar in the hot coffee and add the water. Allow to cool slightly, then pour into an ice-cream machine and churn to a light and fluffy granita.

If you don't have an ice-cream machine, pour the mixture into a shallow tray and place in the freezer. Every 1–2 hours take it out of the freezer and stir with a fork to mix the frozen crystals back into the liquid. When the granita is completely frozen, break it up roughly and place in a food processor. Pulse briefly until it is light and fluffy then return to the freezer until ready to serve. Spoon the granita into glasses and top with whipped cream.

Serves 4

Granita

AL *Gelso*

MULBERRY GRANITA

300 g (10½ oz) ripe,
dark-red mulberries

juice of 1 organic lemon

125 g (4 oz) caster
(superfine) sugar

100 ml (3½ fl oz) water

whipped cream to serve

This granita is the most intense dark-red colour and looks
spectacular topped with whipped cream.

Put all the ingredients except the cream into a food processor
and blend to a smooth purée.

Pour into an ice-cream machine and churn to a light and
fluffy granita.

If you don't have an ice-cream machine, pour the mixture into a
shallow tray and place in the freezer. Every 1–2 hours take it out
of the freezer and stir with a fork to mix the frozen crystals back
into the liquid. When the granita is completely frozen, break it
up roughly and place in a food processor. Pulse briefly until it is
light and fluffy then return to the freezer until ready to serve.

Spoon the granita into glasses and top with whipped cream.

Serves 4

Granita

AL *Limone*

LEMON GRANITA

5 organic lemons

3 lemon leaves

200 g (7 oz) caster (superfine) sugar

200 ml (7 fl oz) water

This granita is quite tart, which is the way I like it. If you prefer it sweeter, just add a little more sugar.

Use a sharp knife to peel 3 thick, long strips of zest from the lemons. Squeeze the lemons and reserve the juice. Place the zest in a saucepan with the lemon leaves, sugar and water and simmer gently for 5 minutes.

Remove from the heat and leave to cool before straining. Stir the lemon juice into the syrup. Pour into an ice-cream machine and churn to a light and fluffy granita.

If you don't have an ice-cream machine, pour the mixture into a shallow tray and place in the freezer. Every 1–2 hours take it out of the freezer and stir with a fork to mix the frozen crystals back into the liquid. When the granita is completely frozen, break it up roughly and place in a food processor. Pulse briefly until it is light and fluffy then return to the freezer until ready to serve. Spoon the granita into glasses and serve.

Serves 6

Mazaresi
LITTLE PISTACHIO CAKES

400 g (14 oz) unsalted
pistachio nuts

300 g (10½ oz) caster
(superfine) sugar

4 organic eggs, separated

grated zest of 1 organic lemon
and the juice of ½ the lemon

½ teaspoon salt

icing (confectioner's) sugar
for dusting

*You can make these little cakes in a medium-sized muffin pan. You
want the individual moulds to be around 5 cm (2 in) in diameter.*
Preheat the oven to 180°C (350°F).

Combine the pistachio nuts and a third of the sugar in a food
processor and pulse to a fine consistency.

In an electric mixer, beat the egg yolks with the rest of the sugar
until very light and fluffy. Add the lemon zest and juice and the
ground pistachio mixture and stir well to combine.

In a separate bowl, whisk the egg whites and salt to stiff peaks
then fold into the batter.

Butter a medium-sized muffin pan and fill the moulds to just
beneath the rim. Transfer to the oven and bake for around
20 minutes. Insert a toothpick to see if they are done.

Remove from the oven and leave to cool on a rack. Gently
remove the cakes from their moulds and dust with icing sugar
before serving.

Makes around 35 cakes

Salina

ISLAND IN THE *Sun*

Opposite: The caper plant in flower

OFF THE NORTHEAST COAST OF SICILY A CLUSTER OF OLD VOLCANOES POKE their heads above the sea. These are the Aeolian Islands, a small world of their own, where Sicily is regarded as a rather foreign place – 'the mainland'. I wanted to go there to visit the island of Salina, which is famous for capers and wine made from the Malvasia grape.

To reach Salina you travel by hydrofoil from the port of Milazzo, passing first the island of Vulcano, where you can smell the sulphur fumes as they vent from the ground, and the island of Lipari, the largest island in the group. You arrive at Salina at the port of Santa Marina. There is a large breakwater for the ferry, a small piazza and a cluster of houses along the waterfront. It's all very small-scale, and as I was to discover later, still looks recognisably as it did one hundred and fifty years ago. Salina is an island that has escaped the blight of mass tourism and sub-standard buildings, mainly because it is so isolated that no-one ever goes there. It survives by neglect.

Our hotel was in the village of Malfa, a fifteen-minute taxi ride away on the far side of the island. The village is perched on a terraced hillside that goes down steeply to a small port. The architecture of the single-storey houses is distinctive

and has not been changed for hundreds of years. Long, low structures look out onto wide terraces that run the full length of each house. Thick masonry pillars hold up shady pergolas. The houses are white with the window surrounds picked out in blue or yellow. The Hotel Signum, where we were staying, is made up of a number of these houses set together like a small village. It is the project of Michele Caruso and his wife Clara Rametta, who want to encourage a different sort of visitor to the island. Their vision is for a sort of tourism that would respect and appreciate Salina's history and traditions, would be small-scale and would leave the existing fabric of the island largely intact. The hotel has a terrace where aperitivi are served in the evening. As you sip your drink, you look out over the Tirrenian Sea to Stromboli, about twenty kilometres away. Like the nearby Mount Etna, Stromboli is an active volcano that emits a puff of white smoke every fifteen minutes or so.

In the hotel dining room, Michele, who is the chef, serves food that draws heavily on the local produce. Capers, tomatoes, figs, almonds and peaches all grow there, and being an island, seafood is abundant. Vincenzo, the sommelier, is passionate and knowledgeable about the local wines, which are made from Nero d'avila or

Malvasia grapes and are sometimes blended with a little of the rare Corinto Nero, a grape variety said to have been brought to the island by the Greeks.

Salina is famous for its capers, which grow over the island in small, rather straggly bushes on the black lava soils. In the spring they have delicate white flowers with violet middles. Salina capers are renowned for being plump and juicy. They are used to add a sharp flavour to a whole range of dishes. There is even a liqueur made from capers. The centre of caper production is the village of Pollara, a little further around the island from Malfa. Pollara is also famous as the village to which Pablo Neruda, the Nobel Prize–winning poet, was exiled in the 1930s. The story of his time there is told in the charming Italian film *Il Postino* (*The Postman*).

As at Ortigia, we decided to see Salina from the water, so took a boat trip around the island. The trip takes a few hours, particularly if you stop for a swim or to admire the sights. Salina has a rocky shoreline, with high cliffs plunging into clear, dark-blue seas. At one point we passed a collection of buoys that formed a large square in the open sea. Out guide informed us that this was a caponada used to catch lambuca, a local fish that looks a little like a mackerel but with a finer flavour.

The caponada is a light platform covered with a blanket of palm fronds. The fronds are weighted so they float several metres below the surface. Apparently the lambuca are attracted to the shade under the fronds and gather there, making them easy to net. Only lambuca can be caught this way and I have not heard about the technique being used anywhere else.

As you look at Salina from the sea, it is remarkable how high up the sides of the two peaks terraces have been created. In many places the terraces look neglected and with little growing there. This is the story of Salina itself. Apparently there were once vines growing on these slopes and a thriving local population who cultivated them. When the scourge of phyloxera hit Europe in the late nineteenth century, Salina was initially spared. As a result, the island prospered at a time when grapes were scarce and sold for high prices. Inevitably phyloxera arrived, the local vines sickened and died and the people, desperately poor, emigrated to survive. The population of Salina today is a fraction of what it was.

At the end of our boat trip we landed at the port of Lingua. Nearby, on the local football field, is a flat area where salt used to be dried and which gave the island its

Above, right: The island of Stromboli by moonlight from the Hotel Signum Terrace

name (from the Italian word 'sale', for salt). Lingua has a small quay and boasts an exceptional bar–gelateria called Bar Alfredo. Out on the piazza down by the water's edge were a number of tables serviced by a shopfront and we sat ourselves down to enjoy the atmosphere. The Bar Alfredo has two specialties – home-made ice creams and sorbets, and a dish they call pane cunzatu – seasoned bread – but which is of their own invention. To describe it as something between a pizza and focaccia bread does not do it justice. Their pane cunzatu was originally created by Alfredo to get around a Euro regulation that restricted him to serving snacks with drinks and not full meals. And this, technically, is what they do. But what arrives at the table is a giant open sandwich of bread, fresh from the oven, split in half, then drizzled in oil and covered with various toppings. Over the years Alfredo and his son, Angelo, who now runs the bar with his brother, have experimented with the toppings. We tried a number and liked them all. To follow I had a sorbetto di gelso, mulberry sorbet, which had a striking purple colour and strong fruity flavour. The Bar Alfredo will continue doing what they have always done despite their success. As Angelo says, 'Una squadra che vince non si cambia,' (You don't change a winning team).

Above: The village of Lingua, Salina

Towards the end of our stay we went to see one of the island's wineries, the Hauner Winery, named after its founder, Carlo Hauner. Carlo arrived on the island in 1962 and set out to restart wine production that had totally collapsed. There were one or two old-timers still making wine for their own use but commercially made Salina wine was non-existent and unknown in the market place. In the 1970s, Hauner wine made from the Malvasia grape began to get noticed in wine shows and in the 1980s Carlo went into full-scale production. Making wine on Salina is something of a challenge. Because of the island location everything costs more and the climate is difficult. The day we visited the winery there was a hot sirocco wind blowing in from Africa and temperatures reached 40°C. But there are areas which have a micro-climate that support the Malvasia vines.

Now that Carlo Hauner has mastered the production of Malvasia grapes on Salina, he is looking for new challenges. He recently established a three-hectare vineyard on lava soil on the island of Vulcano, where vines have never been grown before. It is called Hiera and has a striking label of a slash of glowing red lava flowing across a black background, designed by his father who is an artist.

As we tasted a number of the Hauner wines, Carlo explained them to us: 'This one should be drunk with fish … this with pasta or meat … and this one' (referring to a splendid reserve Malvasia) 'should be drunk with a beautiful girl!'

Salina is a small world of its own. The local people like visitors to come and appreciate it, but not to change it. Their attitude is like the Slow Food movement when it encourages an individual producer. In the case of Salina, however, they want to apply the Slow Food principal to a whole community and already they are succeeding in making the experience for the visitor a special one. My hope is that this approach also works well for the people who live on the island and that young people will be able to continue the traditions and not feel they have to move elsewhere to make a career.

We ate many delicious things on Salina and following is a selection of recipes that remind me of my time there.

Firstly there are two recipes using local seafood that are ideal as starters. Tartar di Acciughe Fresche is a tartare of fresh raw anchovies, and Insalata di Polipini e Seppioline is a salad of baby octopus and baby calamari.

Above and opposite:
At the Hauner winery
with Carlo Hauner
(above left)

Swordfish is one of the high points of Sicilian cooking and I have included another lovely recipe for Involtini di Pesce Spada, this one with citrus flavours.

Croquette di Cipolla are small potato croquettes made with onions and salty capers. They are baked rather than fried and come out of the oven an enticing golden colour.

I have included a recipe for the famous Pane Cunzato from Bar Alfredo with your choice of three different toppings.

At the Hotel Signum we enjoyed a memorable light ravioli stuffed with zucchini flowers, ricotta and mint. I have named this Ravioli di Michele after its creator, who showed me how to make it. My version is slightly different from Michele's – he does not use eggs in the pasta mix, but I prefer them.

For dessert I have included Crostata alla Marmellata di Arance, an orange marmalade tart. Sicily is a great producer of citrus and to me, the bitter-sweet flavour of the marmalade is symbolic of the island as a whole.

Tartar

DI ACCIUGHE *Fresche*

TARTARE OF FRESH ANCHOVIES

4 very fresh anchovies

½ Spanish onion,
very finely diced

1 tablespoon pine nuts, toasted

1 teaspoon currants

a few wild fennel sprigs
(or the feathery green fronds
of farmed fennel)

finely grated zest and juice
of 1 organic lemon

1 small red chilli, finely
sliced (scrape out some of the
seeds to reduce the heat)

4 teaspoons capers
in brine, drained

salt flakes

This intensely flavoured dish makes a wonderful starter served
with crusty bread.

Scale the anchovies then remove the head and backbone.

Make sure there are no bones left.

Dice the anchovies and place them in a mixing bowl with the
other ingredients. Mix together gently, then taste and adjust to
your liking. Serve straight away or refrigerate until needed.

Serves 4 as a starter

Croquette DI *Cipolla*

ONION CROQUETTES

4 medium potatoes, boiled

60 ml (2 fl oz) full-cream milk

2 organic eggs

40 g (1½ oz) capers

salt and pepper

3 medium onions, peeled
and steamed until tender

36 anchovy fillets in oil,
drained and patted dry

130 g (4 oz) fresh breadcrumbs

75 ml (2½ fl oz)
virgin olive oil

These tasty croquettes are delicious as an accompaniment to grilled fish or meat dishes.

Preheat the oven to 200°C (400°F).

Peel the potatoes and push them through a potato ricer or a mouli. In a small jug, mix together the milk, eggs and capers then fold into the potato purée. Season to taste, but be lenient with the salt as the anchovies are themselves salty.

Chop the onions into small pieces and add to the purée. Mix together well. Take spoonfuls of the mixture and shape into 3 cm (1¼ in) balls. Push an anchovy into the centre of each, sealing it in completely.

In a small dish, mix the breadcrumbs and olive oil together. Roll the croquettes in the breadcrumb mix so they are evenly coated. Arrange the croquettes on a lightly oiled oven tray. Bake for around 15–20 minutes, or until they turn golden brown. Serve them straight away.

Makes around 36 croquettes

Insalata

DI POLIPINI E *Seppioline*

OCTOPUS AND CALAMARI SALAD

6 small octopus
(about 15 cm (6 in) in length)
6 small calamari
2 tablespoons red-wine vinegar
2 fresh bay leaves
finely grated zest and juice
of 1 organic lemon
125 ml (4 oz) virgin olive oil
1 celery heart, sliced into
1 cm (½ in) pieces
(including the small leaves)
salt flakes and freshly
ground black pepper

Clean the octopus by cutting off the head and eyes and removing the inside of the sack, then push the beak out through the legs and discard it.

Separate the tentacles from the calamari tubes. Slice the long body tubes open and remove the insides. Don't forget to pull out the long piece of clear cartilage from the tubes as well.

Place the vinegar and bay leaves in a large saucepan of water and bring it to the boil.

Add the octopus and calamari (including tentacles) and boil for 10–15 minutes on a medium heat. Remove the pan from the heat and leave them to cool down in the water.

In a serving bowl, whisk together the lemon zest, juice and olive oil to form an emulsion. Stir in the celery.

Remove the octopus and calamari from the water and peel off the skin. Pull the legs apart and slice the bodies into thick strips. Pat everything dry on kitchen paper and add to the serving bowl. Season with salt flakes and pepper and toss everything together gently. I like to eat this salad at room temperature, as a starter.

Serves 4

Involtini

DI PESCE SPADA AI *Agrumi*

ROLLED SWORDFISH WITH CITRUS

4 slices of swordfish, around 20 cm (8 in) square x 5 mm (¼ in) thick

50 g (2 oz) fresh breadcrumbs

salt and pepper

1 organic lemon, thinly sliced

handful fresh bay leaves

80 ml (3 fl oz) virgin olive oil

STUFFING

grated zest of 1 organic lemon

grated zest of 1 organic orange

2 fresh lemon or orange leaves (make sure they are young and tender)

80 g (3 oz) pecorino piccante, grated

1 small red chilli, seeded (optional)

2 tablespoons virgin olive oil

30 g (1 oz) fresh breadcrumbs

Swordfish is one of the joys of Sicilian cooking and this recipe comes from Salina. You can serve these little swordfish rolls hot or at room temperature.

Preheat the oven to 200°C (400°F).

Use a sharp knife to cut the swordfish slices in half so you have 8 x 10 cm (4 in) slices in total. Pat them dry on kitchen paper.

To make the stuffing, place all the ingredients into a food processor and pulse briefly to combine.

Lay the swordfish slices out on a work surface and top each with a teaspoon of the stuffing. Roll up and secure with a toothpick.

Scatter the breadcrumbs out on your work surface and roll the involtini in the crumbs so they are evenly coated.

Butter an ovenproof dish. Arrange the involtini in the dish and season lightly with salt and pepper. Tuck lemon slices and bay leaves in between the involtini, alternating between the two, then drizzle on the oil. Bake for 10–15 minutes. Any leftover stuffing mixture can be sprinkled over the fish as you serve it.

Serves 4

Pane

Cunzato

OPEN SANDWICH

PANE

1 large piece of focaccia per person
(around 20 cm (8 in) diameter

virgin olive oil

small red chillies, finely chopped

oregano leaves

sea salt

EOLIAN TOPPING

ripe baby tomatoes, halved

capers and pitted olives

1 small Spanish onion, thinly sliced

anchovy fillets in oil

fresh basil leaves

MISTO TOPPING

ripe tomatoes, thinly sliced

capers and pitted olives

grilled eggplant slices

dried tomatoes

fresh mozzarella balls, broken
into small pieces

tuna in oil, drained

SALINA TOPPING

Caper and Almond Pesto (page 118)

ripe tomatoes, diced

grilled eggplant slices

cucunci (caper-berry flowers)

baked ricotta, grated

fresh mint leaves

The original pane cunzato (which means 'seasoned bread') was made by taking bread still warm from the oven, drizzling on some virgin olive oil, then topping with slices of fresh tomato, some fresh oregano and a sprinkling of salt.

These versions are a house specialty at Bar Alfredo — a famous bar-gelateria in Salina. Alfredo and his son created them to get around the local regulation that only allows him to serve snacks with drinks, not full meals. The pane cunzato are like enormous open sandwiches and they make an amazing and satisfying lunch!

I haven't given any measurements because these are very individual sandwiches and you can use as many or as few of the suggested topping ingredients as you like. There are no set rules.

Preheat your grill to medium–high. If the focaccia is very thick, split it in half horizontally. Spread the foccaccia with virgin olive oil then top with chopped chilli, oregano leaves and salt to taste. Place the foccaccia under the grill for a few minutes until it turns golden brown. Pile on the topping of your choice and eat straight away.

Ravioli DI *Michele*

MICHELE'S RAVIOLI

PASTA DOUGH

400 g (14 oz) semolina flour
(hard durum flour)

4 organic eggs

1–2 teaspoons salt

STUFFING

15 zucchini flowers (bitter
stamens removed), chopped

400 g (14 oz) fresh
full-cream ricotta

100 g (3½ oz) freshly
grated Parmiggiano

1 handful fresh mint
leaves, finely chopped

salt and pepper

SAUCE

125 ml (4 oz) virgin olive oil

125 ml (4 oz) water

15–20 zucchini flowers (bitter
stamens removed), finely sliced

1 handful fresh mint
leaves, finely sliced

150 g (5 oz) freshly
grated Parmiggiano

freshly ground black pepper

Michele Caruso from the Hotel Signum showed me how to make these delicious, delicately flavoured ravioli. Michele does not use eggs in the pasta dough because he says the ravioli are lighter. However I actually prefer the consistency of pasta made with egg, so here I give you my version.

Put the flour, eggs and salt into a food processor or electric mixer and mix with a dough hook until the pasta is smooth and elastic (about 5 minutes). Divide the dough into quarters and feed them through a pasta machine, working from the widest setting down to the second-finest setting. Sprinkle the pasta sheets with a little flour and set aside.

To make the stuffing, mix all the ingredients together then taste and adjust the seasoning to your liking. Be careful with the salt, though, as the cheese is already salty.

Use an 8 cm (3 in) pastry cutter to cut out circles from the pasta dough. Place a heaped teaspoon of stuffing in the middle of each, then fold the dough in half over the stuffing and press firmly around the edges to seal.

Bring a large saucepan of salted water to the boil. Add the ravioli carefully and boil for 2 minutes until they float to the surface – they should still be al dente. Lift the ravioli out with a slotted spoon and transfer them to a warm serving dish.

To make the sauce, whisk the oil and water together to form an emulsion. Add the remaining ingredients then pour the sauce over the ravioli and serve immediately.

Serves 6

Crostata

ALLA MARMELLATA DI *Arance*

ORANGE MARMALADE TART

250 g (9 oz) good-quality
bitter marmalade
(home-made is best)

PASTRY

200 g (7 oz) unbleached
plain flour

100 g (3½ oz) unsalted butter
at room temperature

3 organic egg yolks

50 g (2 oz) caster
(superfine) sugar

pinch of salt

grated zest of 1 organic lemon

This is one of my favourite recipes as the pastry is very thin and crunchy and the marmalade is strong and bitter. Any occasion to eat it is perfect.

To make the pastry, put all the ingredients into a food processor and pulse in quick bursts. When the dough is well amalgamated, roll it into a ball and place it in the refrigerator to rest for 30 minutes.

Preheat the oven to 200°C (400°F) and butter a 23 cm (9 in) pie dish.

Roll the pastry out on a lightly floured work surface, keeping a little for the decoration. Lift the pastry onto the buttered pie dish and trim the edges to fit. Spread the marmalade over the base. Use the remaining pastry to cut out little decorations and arrange them on the marmalade. Bake on the bottom shelf of the oven for 20–25 minutes.

Serves 6

Lunch AT *Rovello*

ONE OF THE GREAT PLEASURES OF TRAVELLING IS ARRIVING HOME AND SHARING the experiences of your trip with others. If you have made a culinary journey, as I did in Sicily, then the best way to do this is to prepare a meal with lots of your favourite dishes from your travels. No amount of words can convey the full experience, but if you prepare food for people they will understand.

Our family home, 'Rovello' (named after the village above the house in Lugano where my father lives), is in Sydney, a city that enjoys a benign climate for most of the year. In front of the house is a broad terrace overlooking the garden with views of the harbour beyond. On the terrace, shaded by a wisteria-covered pergola, is a long dining table. Whenever possible, this is where we eat. In particular we have a tradition of a family lunch on Sundays.

In spring, lunching outside can be a bit hit or miss as the weather can be so variable. But on a good day, with the sun shining and beginning to shed some warmth and the first wisteria blossoming on the pergola above, the whole experience can be wonderful. As luck would have it, for my 'Spring in Sicily' lunch we had just such a day.

When I think about the food of Sicily it is the incredible variety of the seafood

Opposite: The family lunch table at 'Rovello' Following pages: Aperitivi (left) and preparing the sfincione (right)

Opposite: Lunch on the table, with swordish salmoriglio in the foreground; Daniel being helpful (top); Jason serving (middle); Samson enjoying his granita with Miranda (bottom)

and vegetable dishes that I find really memorable. The desserts and cakes are memorable too, of course, but that is another story. So on the morning of my Sunday lunch I was up and about early to go to our extraordinary local fish market. There I found beautiful swordfish and some very fresh baby octopus and squid. At my local fruit and vegetable shop, I found wonderful tender radicchio and very young potatoes and leeks.

Whenever I prepare a special lunch such as this, I like to cook a number of different dishes and put them on the table all at once. They get sampled and passed around from person to person. It's very convivial and a great way to try a number of different flavours – everyone can choose their favourites.

In my family, helping with the preparation is very much part of the lunch. Everyone likes to join in, and on that particular day I had many helpers, including my fifteen-month-old grandson. It was so hard to choose which dishes we would try; the truth is I would have loved to cook all of them – and maybe I will over a number of Sundays to come.

This is the menu I chose for my 'Spring in Sicily' lunch. It brought back all sorts of memories for me and gave everyone a taste what makes the food in Sicily so special.

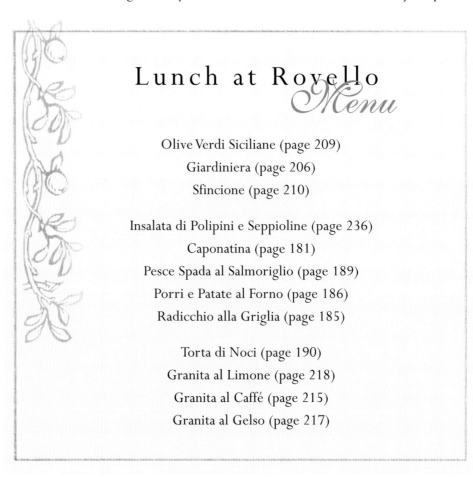

Lunch at Rovello
Menu

Olive Verdi Siciliane (page 209)
Giardiniera (page 206)
Sfincione (page 210)

Insalata di Polipini e Seppioline (page 236)
Caponatina (page 181)
Pesce Spada al Salmoriglio (page 189)
Porri e Patate al Forno (page 186)
Radicchio alla Griglia (page 185)

Torta di Noci (page 190)
Granita al Limone (page 218)
Granita al Caffé (page 215)
Granita al Gelso (page 217)

INDEX OF PLACES

CAFFÈS, BARS AND RESTAURANTS

Pasticceria del Massimo
Amato
Via A. Favara 14/16
Palermo
Tel: 091 333 223
www.pasticceriadelmassimo.com

Pasticceria Mazzara
Via Gen. Magliocco 19
Palermo
Tel: 091 321 443

Pasticceria Chantilly
Corso Umberto 1, 76
Modica
Tel: 0932 941 771
www.pasticceriachantilly.com

Panificio S. Antonio
Via Gianforma P.M. 6
Frigintini (Modica)
Tel: 0932 901 061

Pasticceria
Grammatico Maria
Via V. Emanuele 14
Erice
Tel: 0923 869 390

Gelateria
Conti Gallenti
Corso Umberto 275
Bronte
Tel: 095 691 165

Ristorante
Pan ta Rei
Via Roma 15
Ortigia
Tel: 0931 661 15
www.ristorantepantarei.it

Ristorante L'Ancora
Via G. Perno 7
Ortigia
Tel: 0931 462 369

Ristorante
'À Lumeredda'
Via S. Lorenzo
Malfa
Tel: 090 984 4130

Trattoria Piccolo Napoli
Piazzetta Mulino al Vento 4
Palermo
Tel: 091 320 431

Kursaal Tonnara
Vergine Maria
Via Bordonaro 9
Palermo
Tel: 091 637 2267
www.kursaaltonnara.it

FOOD AND WINE SUPPLIERS

Titone Azienda Agricola
Via Piro 68
Loco Grande
Trapani
Tel: 0923 989 426
www.titone.it

La Casa del Tonno
Via Roma 12
Favignana
Tel: 0923 922 227

Saltworks
Saline Ettore e Infersa
C. da Ettore Infersa 158
Marsala
Tel: 0923 966 936
www.salineettoreinfersa.com

Cantine Florio
Via Vincenzo Florio 1
Marsala
Tel: 0923 781 306
www.cantineflorio.it

'Passopisciaro' Wines
Castiglione
Tel: 0942 983 225
www.passopisciaro.com

Hauner Carlo
Azienda Agricola
Via Umberto 1
Lingua/Salina
Tel: 090 984 3141
www.hauner.it

Spices
Antonio Drago
Via Emanuele de Benedictus
Ortigia

La Cantinaccia
Via XX Settembre 13
Ortigia
Tel: 0931 659 45

PALAZZI

Palazzo Conte Federico
Via dei Biscottari 4
Palermo
www.contefederico.com

ACCOMMODATION

Hotel
Principe di Villafranca
Via G. Turrisi Colonna 4
Palermo
Tel: 091 611 8523

Bed and Breakfast
Ai Lumi
Corso Vittorio Emanuela 71/77
Trapani
Tel: 0923 872 418
www.ailumi.it

Agriturismo
Baglio Vajarassa
C. da Spagnola
Marsala
Tel: 0923 968 628

Agriturismo
Borgo San Nicolao
Randazzo
Tel: 095 924 084
www.borgosannicolao.it

Hotel
Villa Schuler
Piazzetta Bastione, Via Roma
Taormina
Tel: 0942 234 81
www.villaschuler.com

Hotel Signum
Via Scalo 15
Malfa/Salina
Tel: 090 984 4222
www.hotelsignum.it

RECIPE INDEX

Manuela Darling-Gansser was born in Lugano, Switzerland. She spent her early childhood years in Iran before returning to school in Zurich. An inveterate traveller and keen linguist she has lived in the USA, Japan, Italy and the UK, and visited other parts of Asia, India and North Africa. Inspired by family traditions, she has been a passionate cook all her adult life. Her successful travel and food books include *Under the Olive Tree*, *Autumn in Piemonte* and *Winter in the Alps*. Her most recent publication is *Top 10: Recipes for the Beginner Home Cook*. She lives with her family in Sydney.

Simon Griffiths is a Melbourne-based photographer whose work appears regularly in many magazines. His recent books include *Maggie's Kitchen*, *Paul Bangay's Garden Design Handbook*, and he is currently working on more food, travel and gardening titles. Simon enjoys eating and travelling and when he is not working he can be found at the dog park running his whippet.